UNIX® System V
Print Service
Administration

Edited by
Sally A. Browning

P T R Prentice Hall
Englewood Cliffs, New Jersey 07632

PRENTICE HALL OPEN SYSTEMS LIBRARY

Editorial/production supervision: *Mary P. Rottino*
Cover design: *Eloise Starkweather*
Manufacturing buyer: *Mary E. McCartney*
Acquisitions editor: *Phyllis Eve Bregman*
Cover Art: *The Ski Lesson* (Miro) 1966. (From Art Source)

 Published by P T R Prentice-Hall, Inc.
A Simon & Schuster Company
Englewood Cliffs, New Jersey 07632

The Publisher offers discounts on this book when ordered
in bulk quantities. For more information, contact:

Corporate Sales Department
P T R Prentice Hall
113 Sylvan Avenue
Englewood Cliffs, NJ 07632

Phone: 201-592-2863
Fax: 201-592-2249

HP and LaserJet are registered trademarks of Hewlett-Packard Company.
PostScript is a registered trademark of Adobe Systems, Inc.
UNIX is a registered trademark of UNIX System Laboratories, Inc. in the USA and other countries.

Printed in the United States of America

10   9   8   7   6   5   4   3   2   1

ISBN: 0-13-016403-8

Prentice-Hall International (UK) Limited, *London*
Prentice-Hall of Australia Pty. Limited, *Sydney*
Prentice-Hall Canada Inc, *Toronto*
Prentice-Hall Hispanoamericana, S.A., *Mexico*
Prentice-Hall of India Private Limited, *New Delhi*
Prentice-Hall of Japan, Inc., *Tokyo*
Simon & Schuster Asia Pte. Ltd., *Singapore*
Editora Prentice-Hall do Brasil, Ltda., *Rio de Janeiro*

Table of Contents

Chapter 3:   Configuring Printers   27

Chapter 4:   Using Menus to Configure Printers   77

Chapter 5:   Customizing the Print Service   93

Chapter 6:   Administering the Printer Service   107

Chapter 7:   Managing the Print Load   119

Chapter 8:   Pre-Printed Forms   **133**

Chapter 9:   Filters   **153**

Chapter 10:   PostScript Printers   **175**

List of Figures

Preface

This book presents the UNIX System V LP Print Service. It covers installation, configuration, and administration of a full-featured print service. The goal of this book is to de-mystify this important UNIX add-on package by providing all the information you need to administer it in one place. There are basic procedures for novice or casual administrators, tuning and troubleshooting hints for more experienced administrators, and guidelines for "rolling your own" for the most sophisticated or ambitious system programmers and system administrators. While the book concentrates on the shell commands that are used to install the print service, to configure it to support your users, systems, and printers, and to keep it running smoothly, we also present the `sysadm` menu interface for those who prefer to use the menu interface.

This book is derived from the *UNIX System V Release 4 System Administrator's Guide* and *UNIX System V Release 4 System Administrator's Guide for Intel Processors* and related manual pages. While you might already have these guides, the material in this book has been rearranged and re-worked, expanded here and contracted there; it retains much of the flavor and many of the words of the original material.

The chapters in the book are arranged in the order you will probably use them if you are starting from scratch with the print service: you have the book in one hand and the LP Print Service package in the other.

▲ Chapter 1, *Overview of the LP Print Service*, presents general information, like the major components of the software, an overview of a print service administrator's duties, and possible system configurations and their implications.

▲ Chapter 2, *Installing the LP Print Service*, talks about installing the software, registering remote systems, setting up access to remote printers, and presents a list of directories and files used by the print service.

▲ Chapter 3, *Configuring Printers*, covers all the parameters that characterize a printer, including the kinds of files it can handle, the existence of mountable print wheels or character sets, the way you will be notified of problems and how to recover from them, the printer port characteristics, etc.

▲ Chapter 4, *Using Menus to Configure Printers*, revisits the topics of the previous chapter, this time using the menu interface to configure printers.

▲ Chapter 5, *Customizing the Print Service*, talks about changing printer port characteristics, adjusting the `terminfo` description of the printer, and modifying the interface program, all simple ways to customize the print service to your environment.

▲ Chapter 6, *Administering the Print Service*, describes the daily housekeeping tasks that a print service administrator can look forward to: starting and stopping the spooling daemon, enabling and disabling printers, accepting and rejecting print requests on printers or classes of printers, mounting forms, print wheels, or character sets, and so on.

▲ Chapter 7, *Managing the Print Load*, talks about strategies and procedures for managing the print queues, including assigning priorities to print requests and to users, changing the priority of a queued request, and holding, releasing, moving, and cancelling requests.

▲ Chapter 8, *Pre-Printed Forms*, describes the LP print service features that support forms, including procedures for defining, modifying, and removing forms, restricting user access to sensitive forms, mounting and aligning forms on a printer.

▲ Chapter 9, *Filters*, presents the file conversion, fault handling, and enhanced printing modes that can be accomplished by filtering print jobs on their way to the printer. You will learn how to add, modify, remove, and write a filter, the difference between *fast* and *slow* filters, and how filters interact with the interface program.

▲ Chapter 10, *PostScript Printers*, describes the support for PostScript printers, including a brief description of the PostScript language, how to configure a PostScript printer, strategies for dealing with PostScript fonts, and filters that provide access to PostScript interpreter capabilities like landscape mode printing, multiple copies, multiple fonts, and enhanced graphics.

▲ Chapter 11, *Troubleshooting*, describes some common problems you might encounter. Each section heading describes a symptom; the accompanying text gives hints on how to fix the problem.

▲ The Quick Reference Guide lists the most frequent tasks a Print service administrator will perform and provides the name of the associated shell command and pointers to the chapters in this book that discuss that topic.

▲ A *Glossary* that defines some terms associated with the print service that may be new to you.

▲ A comprehensive *Index*.

Related Reading

UNIX System V Programmer's Reference Manual: *Operating System API* (ISBN: 0-13-957549-9), UNIX System Laboratories, Prentice Hall, Englewood Cliffs, NJ.

UNIX SVR4 System Administrator's Guide (ISBN: 0-13-947086-7), UNIX System Laboratories, Prentice Hall, Englewood Cliffs, NJ

UNIX SVR4 System Administrator's Guide for Intel Processors (ISBN: 0-13-879438-3), UNIX System Laboratories, Prentice Hall, Englewood Cliffs, NJ

UNIX SVR4 User's Reference Manual/System Administrator's Reference Manual (Commands a-l, ISBN: 0-13-951310-8; Commands m-z, ISBN: 0-13-951328-0), UNIX System Laboratories, Prentice Hall, Englewood Cliffs, NJ

UNIX System V Programmer's Guide: *Networking Interfaces* (ISBN: 0-13-947078-6), UNIX System Laboratories, Prentice Hall, Englewood Cliffs, NJ

UNIX System V System Files and Devices Reference Manual (ISBN: 0-13-951302-7), UNIX System Laboratories, Prentice Hall, Englewood Cliffs, NJ

PostScript Language Reference Manual, Adobe Systems Inc., Addison-Wesley, Reading, MA, 1985

The Prentice Hall titles are available at all better bookstores or call (800) 922-0579 or (515) 284-2607.

Conventions

The following notational conventions are used in the text:

Italics   represent placeholders in commands and options for context-
                       sensitive values like files names, device types and names,
                       numeric values, etc. Chapter and section names are italicized
                       when referenced in the text as well.

`Courier`   is used for literal commands and options, and output from
                       the computer. Names of menus in the menu interface are also
                       set in `Courier` type.

◆ *Note*   Notes contain remarks slightly off the subject at hand but still perti-
                       nent to the discussion.

▼ *Caution*   Cautions are used to warn you of potential quicksand.

Finally, several of the chapters include a section called *More about command*,
where *command* is one of the commands used in installing, configuring, or
administering the LP print service (e.g., *More about* `lpadmin` in Chapter 3 or
More about `lpfilter` in Chapter 9). These sections discuss the command in
terms of its options rather than the task-oriented presentation of the preceding sections of the chapter. Use them as a reference when you need to look up
the details of a particular option or set of options, or as a quick review of the
full set of capabilities of the command.

Acknowledgments

The book was assembled by converting `troff` files to FrameMaker 3.0 and creating a set of layout templates on a Sun Workstation. These were transferred via `uucp` to FrameMaker 3.0 on a Macintosh, where I created the tables, figures, preface, glossary, and index, and reorganized and rewrote the text, adding material and examples as needed. And, of course, played around with the layout templates. Then the book was sent back to Prentice Hall using `uucp` to FrameMaker on a Sun Workstation for proofing and on to a PC-based FrameMaker for production work.

My thanks to Phyllis Eve Bregman, my editor at Prentice Hall, for suggesting the book and providing me with the initial documentation, and to Dorothy Chang, Dick Hamilton, and Bill Klinger from UNIX System Laboratories for their continuous support during this project. I would also like to thank Mary Fox, Jason Levitt, Ned Pierce, and John Van Dyk for reviewing the manuscript, and Sarah Griffis and Michelle Moore, my baby-sitters. Thanks also to my husband, Bart N. Locanthi, Jr. and our three children, Jennifer, John, and David, for their patience and understanding when I disappear into my office for a few weeks.

Sally A. Browning
October 1992

1

Overview of the LP Print Service

❑ Introduction

The LP print service, originally called the LP spooler, is a set of software utilities that allows you, minimally, to send a file to be printed while you continue with other work. The term "spool" is an acronym for "**simulta-neous peripheral output on-line**," and "LP" originally stood for Line Printer, but has come to include many other types of printing devices. The print service has many optional enhancements: you can make your print service as simple or as sophisticated as you like.

A print service consists of both hardware and software. A minimum system has one computer and one printer and can be expanded to include any number of computers and printing devices. The software consists of the LP print service utilities and optional filters (programs that process the data in a file before it is printed). Filters allow users to print files in one format on a printer that accepts another format (e.g., printing device-independent `troff` output on a PostScript printer) or to vary the output (e.g., printing the pages in reverse order). Depending on the capabilities of the printers, the print service will also manage fonts or print wheels, and provide access to pre-printed forms such as letterhead, invoices, and checks.

What the Print Service Software Is

The System V LP Print Service software has four main components:

▲ user commands

- `lp` submits print requests

- `lpstat` reports on the status of specific printers and print requests

- `cancel` removes requests from the print queue

▲ a server process, `lpsched`, that runs in the background (a *system daemon*) and removes print requests from the print queue, sending the data to the appropriate destination

▲ administrative commands

- `accept` and `reject` control the ability of users to choose destination printers and printer classes

- `enable` and `disable` activate and deactivate individual printers and printer classes

- `lpadmin` controls the printer configurations

- `lpsystem` sets up communications with remote systems

- `lpshut` stops the print service

- `lpfilter` and `lpforms` control the filter and pre-printed forms definitions

- `lpmove` moves print requests from one destination to another

- `lpusers` sets and changes priority limits in the print queue

▲ a spooling directory `/usr/spool/lp/request/`*printer* for each printer or class of printers connected to a given machine. By default, the file to be printed is not copied to the spool directory.

What the Print Service Software Does

Whether your print service is simple (consisting of one computer and one printer that prints every file in the same format on the same type of paper, for example) or a sophisticated one (such as a computer network with multiple printers and a choice of printing formats and forms), the LP software helps you maintain it by performing several important functions:

▲ Scheduling the print requests of multiple users

▲ Scheduling the work of multiple printers

▲ Starting programs that interface with the printers

▲ Filtering users' files (if necessary) so they will be printed properly

▲ Keeping track of the status of jobs

▲ Keeping track of forms and print wheels currently mounted and alerting you to mount needed forms and print wheels

▲ Alerting you to printer problems.

The UNIX system offers a set of menus that help you do these administrative tasks. To invoke the `Printer Services` menu for the LP print service shown in Figure 1-1, type `sysadm` and select the `printers` entry from the main `System Administration` menu:

```
2 Line Printer Services Configuration and Operation
----------------------------------------------------
classes     - Group Related Printers into Classes
filters     - Define Filters for Special Processing
forms       - Define Pre-Printed Forms
operations  - Operate the Print Service
printers    - Configure Printers for the Printer Service
priorities  - Assign Print Queue Priorities to Users
reports     - Report on the Status of the Print Service
requests    - Examine and Manipulate Print Requests
systems     - Configure Connections to Networked Print Services
preSVR4     - Printer Setup
```

Figure 1-1: The `Printer Services` *Menu. This menu is presented when you select printers from the* `sysadm` *menu. Use it to accomplish typical printer administration tasks. You can perform the same tasks by typing commands directly at the shell.*

If you prefer not to use the menus, you can perform the same administrative tasks by issuing commands directly to the shell. The following table shows which shell commands are available for doing the tasks listed on the menu.

Figure 1-2: Shell Commands for Administering the Print Service.
These commands are described in detail in later chapters. On-line and printed manual pages are delivered with the System V LP Print Service package as well.

Task Description	Menu Item	Shell Command
Group printers into classes	classes	lpadmin(1M)
Provide pre-processing soft-ware for files to be printed	filters	lpfilter(1M)
Define pre-printed forms for print requests	forms	lpforms(1M)
Control (turn on/off) queuing of requests; enable & disable printers; mount forms and fonts; start & stop print service; and report status of printers, classes, & forms	operations	accept & reject [*see* accept(1M)], enable & disable [*see* enable(1)], lpadmin(1M), lpsched & lpshut [*see* lpsched(1M)], lpstat(1)
Configure printers for print service	printers	lpadmin(1M)
Define levels of priority avail-able to users requesting print jobs	priorities	lpusers(1M)
Identify active printers, print wheels & character sets, mounted forms, and pending requests	reports	lpstat(1)
Submit and cancel print requests	requests	lp & cancel [*see* lp(1)], lpmove [*see* lpsched(1M)]
Set up communication to remote print service	systems	lpsystem(1M)

❑ Suggestions for LP Print Service Administration

As administrator of the print service, you will

▲   install the software

▲   provide detailed descriptions of each printer

▲   decide which printers will be connected to each system and how the connection will be made

▲   group printers together into classes to enforce a priority scheme or to make a pool of comparable printers appear as a single resource.

▲   manage the print load

▲   start and stop the print service, enable and disable printers, and handle printer alerts like paper outages, paper jams, print wheel and form mount requests, etc.

▲   decide which users will be allowed to help you administer the service and the printers

These tasks will be addressed in later chapters of the book. Before you dive into the nitty gritty details, though, take a few minutes to list your printers, systems, and general requirements and expectations of a print service.

Configuring Your Printer Sites

Where you decide to put your printers and how you decide to connect them to your computers depends on how those printers will be used. There are three possible scenarios: (1) users may access printers attached to their own computer; (2) users may access printers attached to a server computer; and (3) users may access remote printers on a network.

▲   You may want to connect a particular printer directly to the computer that is the home machine of the users who will use that printer most often. If you do, the type of connection you have will be referred to as a direct connection. An environment that includes more than one computer, each of which has a direct connection to a printer, is said to have a *distributed printing configuration*, as shown in Figure 1-2(a).

▲ You may want to have all your printers in one physical location, such
   as a computer center. If so, you might connect them all to one computer. Users on other computers who want to use a printer may
   access it through a network linking their own computers to the computer serving the printers. An environment in which one computer
   serves several printers (which can be accessed only through a com-
   puter-to-computer network) is described as a *print server configuration*
   and is shown in Figure 1-3(b).

▲ You may want to link most of your printers to a dedicated printer
   server computer, while allowing other printers to be connected to
   your machine. If so, you can arrange your computers and printers in
   a *network printing configuration*, as shown in Figure 1-3(c).

Whatever strategy you choose, remember that it is not cast in concrete. As
you gain experience with the software and the print load, you can move
printers around as needed.

The rest of the book describes the tasks that are required of a print server
administrator. Topics include the following:

▲ Installation procedures, including a list of directories and files delivered as part of the package

▲ Configuration procedures that will help you tailor the print service to
   the unique requirements of your users, systems, and printers.

▲ Suggestions, guidelines, and procedures for administering your print
   service

▲ Instructions for supporting PostScript printers

▲ Instructions for writing customized filters and interface programs

▲ Suggestions, guidelines, and procedures for supporting pre-printed
   forms

▲ Troubleshooting guidelines

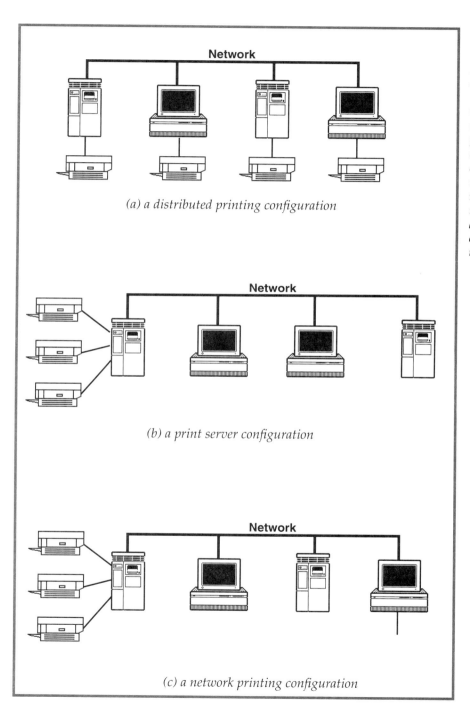

(a) a distributed printing configuration

(b) a print server configuration

(c) a network printing configuration

Figure 1-3: Possible Printing Configurations. *Printers can be distributed throughout the network, concentrated on a single print server, or configured as a combination of the two. Your configuration will reflect the unique goals and requirements of your users, systems, and printers.*

2

Installing the LP Print Service

❏ **Overview**

This chapter covers

- ▲ installing the System V LP Print Service software
- ▲ supporting distributed, server, and network printing configurations, including
  - • installing the print service on server machines
  - • installing user and administrative commands (but not the spooling daemon `lpsched`) on the client machines
  - • registering clients and servers with the print service
- ▲ defining a default destination printer
- ▲ a listing of the directories and files that comprise the LP print service

Your first tasks are to physically connect your printers to your computers and to install the LP print service utilities from the floppy diskettes on which they were delivered. Once installed, these utilities will be available whenever your UNIX system is brought up.

◆ *Note*   A prerequisite for using the LP package is to have the Basic Network Utilities (BNU) package installed. This exists on a separate package in your installation set and is installed like the LP package[1].

The following documentation can be of specific help in the area of software and printer installation:

▲ The installation guide that was delivered with print service package

▲ The installation manual that was delivered with your printer

▲ `terminfo`(4) in the *System Files and Devices Reference Manual*

For details about how to order any of these books, see *Related Reading* in the *Preface* at the beginning of this book.

❏ Installing the LP Print Service

◆ *Note*   Before you can install the LP print service software, you must be logged in as `root`, and the system must be in multi-user or single-user state. (If you are in single-user state, you must run the command `mount /usr` before following this procedure.)

The LP package is an add-on to the base UNIX software. It consists of one or more floppy diskettes or tapes in the installation set.

▲ Connect your printer (and any optional hardware you may have) to your computer, following the instructions in the appropriate documents.

▲ Install the LP print service software by executing the following command:

----

1. The Basic Network Utilities supports dial-up lines and may be sufficient for your needs. The Network Services Utilities support high-speed local-area networks and will provide access to remote systems, printers, and users.

```
pkgadd -d diskette1
```

The `pkgadd` command will prompt you to insert the first of the floppy diskettes labeled "LP Spooling Utilities" into the diskette drive at the appropriate time. You will be prompted through the whole installation process.

Controlling Access to the Print Service

Any user can send requests to the LP print service, check the status of requests, and cancel requests. In addition, you may want to give your users the ability to disable and enable a printer by authorizing them to use the `enable` and `disable` commands. The advantage in doing so is that a user with this authority can turn off a malfunctioning printer without calling the administrator. On the other hand, it may not be reasonable to allow regular users to disable printers in your printing environment.

During the installation process, the `pkgadd` command will ask you whether you want to authorize the users on your system to enable and disable the printer.

For further instructions on authorizing and restricting access to the `enable` and `disable` commands, see *Allowing Users to Enable and Disable a Printer* in the next chapter.

❑ Sharing Printers

The LP print service software should be installed on each system that has a printer connected to it, using the procedure given above. In addition, you can allow users on remote systems to submit print requests. Thus, users with no local printer can still generate printed output, and everyone on the network can access a printer with special capabilities, like a high-resolution image setter.

In the discussions that follow, the *server* is any machine that will provide print service to remote users. The *client* is the remote system that desires access to a server's printers.

If you have access to other systems through the Remote File Sharing Utilities (RFS), you may want to share printers with those systems by running the print service over RFS. You can do so by following these instructions.

On the print server machines:

1. Set up the LP print service on the server as you would on any machine. Make sure that the printer works and that you are able to print text on it.

2. Share `/var/spool/lp`, `/etc/lp`, and `/var/lp` with all the client(s) that will be using this printer.

3. In `/etc/rfs/auth.info/uid.rules`, map the user ID (UID) of `lp` to itself, so the entry in `uid.rules` appears as follows:

        map lp

On the client machines:

1. Do not run the scheduler on the client machines. You need only `lp`, `lpstat`, and other LP print service commands.

2. Mount the resources that were shared by the server on the client's `/var/spool/lp`, `/etc/lp`, and `/var/lp`.

On client machines, the `-c` option of `lp` should be used for any user file not in a shared resource. This will force a copy of the file to be sent to the server machine. The LP print service cannot access local files that are not in a shared resource.

❑ What's Next?

Even though you've connected the hardware and installed the software, printers will not be available for use immediately. Before users can start submitting requests for print jobs, you must complete the following three steps:

▲   You must *configure* your printers; that is, you must name the printers and describe their characteristics to the print service.

▲ You must *register* printer and printer classes so that the print service can accept and queue print requests for that printer or class.

▲ You must *enable* your printers to make them available to users.

Configuring and enabling a printer is discussed in the next chapter; classes are described in Chapter 4. Information on registering both local and remote printers for access by both local and remote users follows.

❏ Allowing Local Users to Access Local Printers

Local printers are configured using the `lpadmin` command, as described in the next chapter. In the process, they are automatically registered with the print service.

❏ Allowing Local Users to Access Remote Printers

◆ *Note*   This section does not apply if you are making only a local printer accessible to users on your system.

A *remote printer* is one that is connected to a system other than your local system. To make a remote printer accessible, the name of the system on which the printer resides must be registered with the print service using the `lpsystem` command. If the remote printer resides on a System V Release 4 machine, enter

    lpsystem *system-name*

If the remote printer resides on a BSD machine, enter

    lpsystem -t bsd *system-name*

In either case, after executing the `lpsystem` command, enter the following `lpadmin` command:

```
lpadmin -p printer -s system-name
```

where *printer* is the name by which your users identify the remote printer and *system-name* is the name of the system on which that printer resides. You can usually use the same name used for that printer on the remote system. If, however, the name used by the remote system is already in use on your system, you must use a different name. To assign a different name to a remote printer, enter the following:

```
lpadmin -p local-name -s system-name!remote-name
```

Example - Renaming a Remote Printer

You want to register a printer called `psjet` that is connected to a remote system called lilac. There is already a printer called `psjet` on your own system so you must give the remote printer a new name, say `laser`. Register the new name by entering the following:

```
lpadmin -p laser -s lilac!psjet
```

Before you add a remote printer to your system, be sure communications between your system and the network have been set up properly, and verified.

❑ Allowing Remote Users to Access Local Printers

◆ *Note*   This section does not apply if you are making only a local printer accessible to users on your system.

Making the printers on your local system accessible to users on remote systems is a two-step process: you must configure the port monitor on the local system and you must register the system with the LP print service. This section provides instructions for these tasks.

Configuring the Local Port Monitor

If the remote system will need access to printers connected directly to your computer, then you need to configure the local port monitor for the network you share to accept service requests and to notify the LP print service of such requests. For System V machines calling your machines, issue the following command:

```
pmadm -a -p netname -s lp -i root -V `nlsadmin -V` \
    -m `nlsadmin -o /var/spool/lp/fifos/listenS5`
```

where *netname* is the name of a network such as `starlan` or `tcp`.

If you expect users on BSD machines to send print requests to your machine, then you need to configure your local port monitor. The output of this command will be a hexadecimal number.

```
pmadm -a -p tcp -s lpd -i root -V `nlsadmin -V` \
    -m `nlsadmin -o /var/spool/lp/fifos/listenBSD \
    -A '\xaddress'`
```

Before issuing this command for a BSD machine, however, you need to know its *TCP/IP address*. To get this address, use the `-A` option with the `lpsystem` command, as follows:

```
lpsystem -A
```

Adding a System Entry

If you want your system to accept jobs from a remote system (and vice-versa), the print service must know about that system. The `lpsystem` command allows you to register remote systems with the local print service. Run the command as follows:

```
lpsystem system-name
```

where *system-name* is the name of the remote system.

❏ More about lpsystem

In the previous sections on registering printers with the print service, you have seen simple examples of the lpsystem command. This section describes all the options and functions available.

The lpsystem command is used to define parameters for the LP print service, with respect to communication (through a high-speed network such as StarLAN or TCP/IP) with remote systems. Only a privileged user (that is, the owner of the login root) may execute the lpsystem command.

Specifically, the lpsystem command is used to identify the remote systems with which the local LP print service can exchange print requests. These remote systems are described to the local LP print service in terms of several parameters that control communication: *type*, *retry*, and *timeout*. These parameters are defined in /etc/lp/Systems. You can edit this file with a text editor such as vi but editing is not recommended.

The legal forms of the lpsystem command are shown below. Table 2-1 describes the command options in more detail.

```
lpsystem [-t type] [-T timeout] [-R retry] \
    [ -y "comment"] system-name [system-name ...]

lpsystem -l [system-name ...]

lpsystem -r system-name [system-name ...]

lpsystem -A
```

Option	Default	Meaning
-A		Print out the TCP/IP address of the local machine in a format to be used when configuring the local port monitor to accept requests from a SunOS system
-l	all	List the LP print service parameters associated with the specified system, or with all known systems if *system-name* is not specified
-R	n	The next argument is n, 0, or *N* and gives the length of time to wait before trying to reestablish a connection with the specified remote system. *N* is a positive integer specifying the number of minutes to wait before trying to reconnect, n means do not attempt to reconnect until there is more work in the queue, and 0 means try to reconnect immediately
-r		Remove *system-name*. The print service will no longer accept jobs from that system, or send jobs to it.
-T	n	The next argument specifies the length of time, in minutes, that the print service should allow a network connection to be idle. If the connection to the remote system is idle (*i.e.*, there is no network traffic) for *N* minutes, the connection is dropped. It will be reestablished when there is more work. Legal values are n, 0, and *N*, where *N* is a positive integer specifying the allowable idle time, n means never time out, and 0 means drop the connection as soon as it is idle.
-t	s5	The next argument is the system type. Two values are accepted: s5 (System V Release 4) and bsd (SunOS)
-y		The next argument is a free form comment string that will be printed whenever lpsystem -l is used.

Figure 2-1: `lpsystem` ***Options.*** *These options define communication parameters for connections to remote printers.*

/etc/lp/Systems contains relatively little information for controlling network communications. Network addresses and services are handled by the Netconfig and Netdir facilities (see the "Network Services" chapter in the *System Administrator's Guide* for a discussion of network addresses and services). Port monitors handle listening for remote service requests and routing the connection to the print service (see the "Service Access" chapter in the *System Administrator's Guide* for a discussion of port monitors).

If the Netconfig and Netdir facilities are not set up properly, out-bound remote print services probably will not work. Similarly, if the local port monitors are not set up to route remote print requests to the print service, then service for remote systems will not be provided.

The print service uses one process for each remote system with which it communicates, and it communicates with a remote system only when there is work to be done on that system or work being sent from that system. The system initiating the connection is the "master" process and the system accepting the connection is the "slave" process. This designation serves only to determine which process dies (the slave) when a connection is dropped, and helps prevent more than one process from communicating with a remote system. All connections are bi-directional, regardless of the master/slave designation. If a master process times out, then both the slave and master will exit. If a slave times out, then it is possible that the master may still live and retry the connection after the retry interval. Therefore, one system's resource management strategy can effect another system's strategy.

A SunOS system (described with `-t bsd`) can be connected to your system only via TCP/IP, and print requests from a SunOS system can come in to your machine only via a special port (515). The address given to you from `lpsystem` will be the address of your system and port 515. This address is used by your TCP/IP port monitor to "listen" on that address and port, and to route connections to the print service. (This procedure is discussed in the "Service Access" chapter of the *System Administrator's Guide*.) The command `lpsystem -A` will not work if your system name and IP address are not listed in `/etc/inet/hosts` and the printer service is not listed in `/etc/inet/services`.

❏ Defining a Default Destination Printer

You can define the printer or class to be used to print a file when the user has not explicitly asked for a particular destination and has not set the `LPDEST` shell variable. The printer or class must already exist.

Make a printer or class the default destination by entering the following command:

```
lpadmin -d printer-or-class-name
```

If you later decide that there should be no default destination, enter a null *printer-or-class-name* as in the following command.

```
lpadmin -d
```

If you don't set a default destination, there will be none. Users will have to explicitly name a printer or class in each print request (unless they specify the -T *content-type* option), or will have to set the LPDEST shell variable with the name of a destination.

❏ Directories and Files Used by LP Print Service

This section lists the directories and files used by the LP print service. You can use this list to see if any files are missing or if the ownership or access permissions have changed. Normal operation of the LP print service should not cause any problems. However, if you do notice any discrepancies, there may be a security breach on your system.

The LP Print service keeps a record of all printing requests, printer alerts, printer faults, etc., in /var/lp/logs/requests. See *Cleaning Out the Request Log* in Chapter 7 for a description of the crontab entry that automatically cleans out the request log periodically.

The various LP print service files and directories are found under the main directories listed below. These main directories should have the access permissions and ownerships shown.

Permissions	Owner	Group	Directory or File
drwxrwxr-x	lp	lp	/var/spool/lp
drwxrwxr-x	lp	lp	/var/lp
drwxrwxr-x	lp	lp	/etc/lp
drwxrw-r-x	root	other	/usr/lib/lp

Figure 2-2: Main Print Service Directories. The major directories used by the print service are owned by user lp.

You can check this by entering the following command:

```
ls -ld /var/spool/lp /var/lp /etc/lp /usr/lib/lp
```

Under these directories you should see only the files and directories shown in the table on the next few pages. You can generate a similar table for comparison by entering this command:

```
ls -lR /var/spool/lp /var/lp /etc/lp /usr/lib/lp
```

Figure 2-3: Dire ctories and Files Used by the LP Print Service.
Here are the access permissions and ownerships for files used by the LP print service. Use it as a guide as you read the rest of this book.

Permissions	Owner	Group	Directory or File
/var/spool/lp:			
-rw-rw-r--	lp	lp	SCHEDLOCK
drwxrwxr-x	lp	lp	admins
lrwxrwxrwx	lp	lp	bin->/usr/lib/lp/bin
lrw-rw-r--	lp	lp	default->/etc/lp/default
drwxrwxr-x	lp	lp	fifos
lrwxrwxr-x	lp	lp	logs->/var/lp/logs
lrwxrwxr-x	lp	lp	model->/usr/lib/lp/model
drwxrwxr-x	lp	lp	requests
drwxrwxr-x	lp	lp	system
lrwxrwxrwx	lp	lp	temp->/var/spool/lp/tmp/sfsti
drwx--x--x	lp	lp	tmp
-rw-r--r--	lp	lp	users->/etc/lp/users
/var/spool/lp/admins:			
lrwxrwxrwx	lp	lp	lp->/etc/lp
/var/spool/lp/fifos:			
prw-rw-rw-	lp	lp	FIFO
prw-------	root	other	listenBSD
prw-------	root	other	listenS5
drwxrwx--x	lp	lp	private
drwxrwx-wx	lp	lp	public
/var/spool/lp/fifos/private:			
pr--------	*user*	*group*	*systemPID*
:			

Permissions	Owner	Group	Directory or File
`/var/spool/lp/fifos/public:`			
`pr--------`	*user*	*group*	*systemPID*
⋮			
`/var/spool/lp/requests:`			
`drwxrwx---`	`lp`	`lp`	*system1*
`drwxrwx---`	`lp`	`lp`	*system2*
⋮			
`drwxrwx---`	`lp`	`lp`	*systemN*
`/var/spool/lp/requests/`*systemK*`:`			
`-rw-rw----`	`lp`	`lp`	*id1*-0
`-rw-rw----`	`lp`	`lp`	*id2*-0
⋮			
`-rw-rw----`	`lp`	`lp`	*idN*-0
`/var/spool/lp/system:`			
`-rw-rw-r--`	`lp`	`lp`	`cstatus`
`-rw-rw-r--`	`lp`	`lp`	`pstatus`
`/var/spool/lp/tmp:`			
`drwxrwxr-x`	`lp`	`lp`	*system1*
`drwxrwxr-x`	`lp`	`lp`	*system2*
⋮			
`drwxrwxr-x`	`lp`	`lp`	*systemN*

Permissions	Owner	Group	Directory or File
/var/spool/lp/tmp/*systemK*:			
-rw-------	lp	lp	*idN*-0
-rw-------	lp	lp	*idN*-1
-rw-------	lp	lp	*idN*-2
⋮			
-rw-------	lp	lp	*idN*-M
-rw-------	lp	lp	F*idN*-1
-rw-------	lp	lp	F*idN*-2
⋮			
-rw-------	lp	lp	F*idN*-M
-rw-------	lp	lp	idN
-rw-------	lp	lp	A-*K*
-rw-------	lp	lp	F-*K*
-rw-------	lp	lp	P-*K*
/var/lp/logs:			
-rw-rw----	lp	lp	lpsched
-rw-rw----	lp	lp	requests
-rw-rw-r--	root	other	lpNetLog
-rw-rw-r--	root	other	p*PID*
-rw-rw-r--	root	other	c*PID*
/etc/lp:			
-rw-rw-r--	lp	lp	Systems
drwxrwxr-x	lp	lp	classes
-rw-rw-r--	lp	lp	filter.table
-rw-rw-r--	lp	lp	filter.table.i
drwxrwxr-x	lp	lp	forms
drwxrwxr-x	lp	lp	interfaces
lrwxrwxrwx	lp	lp	logs->/var/lp/logs
drwxrwxr-x	lp	lp	printers
drwxrwxr-x	lp	lp	printwheels
-rw-rw-r--	lp	lp	users

Permissions	Owner	Group	Directory or File
/etc/lp/classes:			
-rw-rw-r--	lp	lp	*class1*
-rw-rw-r--	lp	lp	*class2*
⋮			
-rw-rw-r--	lp	lp	*classN*
/etc/lp/forms:			
drwxrwxr-x	lp	lp	*form1*
drwxrwxr-x	lp	lp	*form2*
⋮			
drwxrwxr-x	lp	lp	*formN*
/etc/lp/forms/*formK*:			
-rwxrwx---	lp	lp	alert.sh
-rw-rw----	lp	lp	alert.vars
-rw-rw----	lp	lp	align_ptrn
-rw-rw-r--	lp	lp	allow
-rw-rw-r--	lp	lp	comment
-rw-rw-r--	lp	lp	deny
-rw-rw-r--	lp	lp	describe
/etc/lp/interfaces:			
-rwxrwxr-x	lp	lp	*printer1*
-rwxrwxr-x	lp	lp	*printer2*
⋮			
-rwxrwxr-x	lp	lp	*printerN*
/etc/lp/printers:			
drwxrwxr-x	lp	lp	*printer1*
drwxrwxr-x	lp	lp	*printer2*
⋮			
drwxrwxr-x	lp	lp	*printerN*

Permissions	Owner	Group	Directory or File
/etc/lp/printers/*printerK*:			
-rwxrwx---	lp	lp	alert.sh
-rw-rw----	lp	lp	alert.vars
-rw-rw-r--	lp	lp	comment
-rw-rw-r--	lp	lp	configuration
-rw-rw-r--	lp	lp	forms.allow
-rw-rw-r--	lp	lp	forms.deny
-rw-rw-r--	lp	lp	residentfonts
-rw-rw-r--	lp	lp	users.allow
-rw-rw-r--	lp	lp	users.deny
/etc/lp/printwheels:			
drwxrwxr-x	lp	lp	*printwheel1*
drwxrwxr-x	lp	lp	*printwheel2*
⋮			
drwxrwxr-x	**lp**	**lp**	*printwheelN*
/etc/lp/printwheels/*printwheelK*:			
-rwxrwx---	lp	lp	alert.sh
-rw-rw----	lp	lp	alert.vars
/usr/lib/lp:			
dr-xr-xr-x	lp	lp	bin
---x--x--x	lp	lp	lpNet
---x--x---	lp	lp	lpdata
---s--x--x	root	lp	lpsched
drwxrwxr-x	lp	lp	model
drwxrwxr-x	lp	lp	postscript
/usr/lib/lp/bin:			
-r--r--r-	lp	lp	alert.proto
-r-xr-xr-x	lp	lp	drain.output
-r-xr-xr-x	lp	lp	lp.cat
-r-xr-xr-x	lp	lp	lp.set
-r-xr-xr-x	lp	lp	lp.tell
-r-xr-xr-x	lp	lp	slow.filter

Permissions	Owner	Group	Directory or File
/usr/lib/lp/model:			
-rwxrwxr-x	lp	lp	standard
/usr/lib/lp/postscript:			
-rwxrwxr-x	lp	lp	download
-rwxrwxr-x	lp	lp	dpost
-rwxrwxr-x	lp	lp	postdaisy
-rwxrwxr-x	lp	lp	postdmd
-rwxrwxr-x	lp	lp	postio
-rwxrwxr-x	lp	lp	postmd
-rwxrwxr-x	lp	lp	postplot
-rwxrwxr-x	lp	lp	postpost
-rwxrwxr-x	lp	lp	postreverse
-rwxrwxr-x	lp	lp	posttek

The italicized names (*printerN*, *formN*, *classN*, *printwheelN*, *idN*, and *systemN*)
are placeholders for a single printer, form, class, print wheel, request ID, and
UNIX system name, respectively (*idN* is just the numeric part of the request
ID). There will be one set of these directories and files for each active printer,
form, class, print wheel and request configured on your system, and for each
system used for remote printing. The italicized letter *K* is a placeholder for an
internal number; the A-*K*, F-*K*, and P-2*K* files are used to store alert messages.

The ownership and permissions of the *idN-M* request files under the
/var/spool/lp/tmp/*systemK* directory will change during the life of a
print request, alternating between the user who submitted the request and
the lp ID.

The two directories under the /var/spool/lp/fifos directory contain
named pipes used to communicate between the LP print service and commands such as lpadmin, lpstat, and lp. These directories must have the
permission flags and ownership shown if communication with the LP print
service is to work. Every entry below these directories is given a unique name
formed by combining the name of the system (the node name) and the process ID of the command. The uniqueness of the entry names prevents two or
more people from accidentally sharing the same communications path.

3

Configuring
Printers

❑ Overview

Before the LP print service can start accepting print requests, you will have to describe the characteristics of each printer you have. While you need to specify very little information to add a new printer to the LP print service, the more information you provide, the better the printer will satisfy the needs of your users.

The following parameters are *required*:

▲ A **printer name**. See *Establishing a Printer Name* later in this chapter.

▲ A **connection method** (for local printers only). See the section *Connecting Printers to Systems*.

▲ A **system name** (for access to remote printers and for allowing remote access to local printers). See *Allowing Local Users to Access Remote Printers* and *Allowing Remote Users to Access Local Printers* in the previous chapter.

The following parameters are not required (that is, they have default values), but should be specified to support the full capabilities of your printer:

▲ A **printer type**. See *Setting the Printer Type* in this chapter.

▲ A **content types**. See *Listing the Content Types*.

▲ The **printer port characteristics**. See *Establishing Printer Port Characteristics* in this chapter.

▲ Lists of available **character sets**, **print wheels**, and **forms**. See *Listing Available Character Sets or Print Wheels* in this chapter. Forms are discussed in Chapter 8.

▲ An **alert method** for mounting print wheels, character sets, and forms. See *Alerting to Mount a Print Wheel* in this chapter. Forms are discussed in Chapter 8, *Pre-printed Forms*.

▲ The **printer fault alerting and recovery** methods. See *Catching Printer Fault Alerts* and *Defining Printer Fault Recovery*.

▲ A **printer description**. See *Adding a Printer Description*.

▲ The **default printing attributes**. See *Setting Default Printing Attributes* in the chapter.

These parameters are also optional. The default values are satisfactory in many environments:

▲ A **class name**. See *Grouping Printers into Classes*.

▲ An **interface program**. See *Defining the Interface Program*.

▲ Restrictions on **user access**. See *Establishing Access Restrictions*.

▲ A **banner page**. See *Including a Banner Page in the Output*.

The descriptions in the sections below will help you understand what this printer configuration information means and how it is used, so that you can decide how to configure your printers. In each section you will also be shown how to specify this information when adding a printer. While you can follow each of the sections in order and correctly configure a printer in several steps, you may want to wait until you've read all the sections before adding a printer, so that you can do it in fewer steps.

This chapter presents the shell commands for configuring printers. There is also a menu interface; it is discussed in the next chapter, *Using Menus to Configure Printers*.

❑ Establishing a Printer Name

The printer name and the connection method (described next) are the only items you must specify to define a new local printer. To define a new remote printer, you must specify the printer name and the system name. The printer name is used to identify the printer, both by you (when you want to change the printer configuration or manage the printer), and by users who want to use the printer. The name may contain a maximum of fourteen alphanumeric characters and underscores.

You may choose any name you like, but it is good practice to choose a name that is meaningful to the users of the LP print service. For example, `laser` is a good name for a laser printer. If you have several laser printers you may name them `laser1`, `laser2`, and so on. Or you might incorporate the printer's location into the name to help users choose the closest one: `lp4C` could name the laser printer on the fourth floor, in corridor C.

You don't have to try to fit a lot of descriptive information into the name; there is a better place for this information (see the *Adding a Printer Description* section below). You also don't have to make the name precisely identify the type of printer; users who need to use a particular type of printer can specify it by type rather than name (see the *Setting the Printer Type* section below).

You will use the printer name every time you want to refer to the printer: when adding other configuration information for the printer, when changing the configuration of the printer, when referring to the status of the printer, and when removing the printer. Thus the first thing you must do to add a printer is identify its name. You will do this as shown below; but don't do it yet because you'll also need to specify the connection method.

```
lpadmin -p printer-name
```

There are no default names; you must give every printer a unique name.

❏ Connecting Printers to Systems

◆ *Note*   This section does not apply if you are making a remote printer
             accessible to users on your system.

The LP print service allows you to connect a printer to your computer in one
of the following three ways:

▲ by connecting the printer directly to your computer

▲ by connecting the printer directly to a network to which your computer is attached

▲ by connecting the printer to a modem

Figure 3-1 shows these three types of connections.

The simplest connection method is by connecting a printer directly to your
computer. You may, however, want to connect a printer to a network (so it can
be shared with other computers or workstations), or to a modem. Whichever
method you use, you must describe it to the LP print service after you've connected the hardware.

To define the connection method for a new printer for your print service, run
the lpadmin command, specifying a connection method through either the
-v option for a directly connected printer or the -U option for a printer
directly connected to a network or a printer connected to a modem.

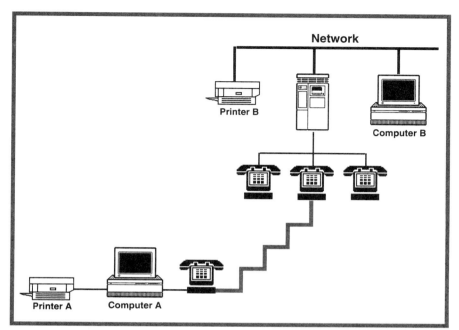

Figure 3-1: Methods of Connecting a Printer to a Computer. *Computer A accesses printer A through a direct connection, and accesses printer B using modems. Computer B accesses printer B over a local area network. Computer B may be able to access printer A through a remote connection.*

In the figure: Network, Printer B, Computer B, Computer A, Printer A.

Direct Connections

The simplest and most common method by which printers are connected to a computer is direct connection. If you use this method, you generally need to specify only two items on the command line when you make the connection: the name of the printer and the name of the connecting port. To connect a printer directly to your computer enter the following command:

```
lpadmin -p printer-name -v pathname
```

where *pathname* is the name of the special device file representing the printer port. The following are examples of typical names of special device files.

```
/dev/contty
/dev/term/11
/dev/term/12
/dev/term/13
/dev/term/14
```

```
/dev/term/15
```

(For details about using these files, see *Establishing Printer Port Characteristics* later in this chapter.)

Using a Printer As a Login Terminal

Some directly connected printers can also be used as terminals for login sessions. If you want to use a printer as a terminal, you must arrange for the LP print service to handle it as such. To do so, use the -l option to the lpadmin command, as follows:

```
lpadmin -p printer-name -v pathname -l
```

As before, *pathname* is the name of the special file representing the printer port. If the -l option is specified, the printer will be disabled automatically whenever the LP print service is started, and therefore will have to be manually enabled before it can be used for printing. For instructions on manually enabling a printer, see *Enabling and Disabling a Printer* later in this chapter.

Connections to Networks and Modems

Why would you want to use a printer that is not directly connected to your computer?

▲ The environment where a printer is located is so far from the computer that a direct connection is not possible or practical. For example, you might have one printer in use with a single terminal at a branch office located a few miles from your main site.

▲ You may want to share a printer with computers that are not on a common network.

▲ You may need to print on a high resolution imagesetter. Since it is an expensive device, one imagesetter is shared by all the users on the network.

The LP print service establishes a connection to a printer when a print request is processed; the connection is dropped when the printing is finished, making the printer available to the next machine that calls it. Thus the printer gets shared by the users of all the computers, more or less equally.

There are two methods for connecting printers that are not directly connected to your system: attached directly to a network and through a dial-up modem. The LP print service uses the Basic Network Utilities (BNU) to handle both methods.

When a modem connection is used, the printer must be connected to a dialed modem, and the dial-out modem must be connected to the computer. Whether printers are connected to a modem or directly to a network, the connection must be described to the BNU.

To make a printer connected in one of these ways available to your users, enter the following command:

```
lpadmin -p printer-name -U dial-info
```

where *dial-info* is either the telephone number to be dialed to reach the printer's modem, or the system name entered in the BNU `Systems` file for the printer.

◆ *Note*   The −U option provides a way to link a single printer to your print service. It does not allow you to connect with a print service on another system.

A note on printers connected to a modem or directly to a network: if the printer or port is busy, the LP print service will automatically retry later. This retry rate is 10 minutes if the printer is busy, and 20 minutes if the port is busy. These rates are not adjustable. However, you can force an immediate retry by issuing an `enable` command for the printer. If the port or printer is likely to be busy for an extended period, you should issue a `disable` command.

The `lpstat -p` command reports the reason for a failed dial attempt. Also, if you are alerted to a dialing fault (see the *Fault Alerting* section below), the alert message will give the reason for the fault. These messages are identical to the error messages produced by the Basic Network Utilities for similar problems.

In summary, to add local printers to your system, run the `lpadmin` command, specifying a connection method through one of two options: the −v option for a directly connected printer, or the −U option for a networked printer.

❑ Setting the Printer Type

A printer type is the generic name for a printer. Typically it is derived from the manufacturer's name, such as 572 for the AT&T 572 Dot Matrix Printer. When you set up your system you can enhance its ability to serve your users by classifying, on the basis of type, the printers available through the print service. Assigning a type for each printer is also important because the LP software extracts information about printers from the terminfo database on the basis of type. This information includes the list of the printer's capabilities that is used to check the configuration information you supply to the print service. (By checking information provided by you against the capabilities of the printer, the print service can catch any inappropriate information you may have supplied.) The terminfo database also specifies the control data needed to initialize a particular printer before printing a file.

You can assign several types to a printer, if your printer is capable of emulating more than one kind of printer. The AT&T 593 Laser Printer, for instance, can emulate an IBM Proprinter XL, an Epson FX86c, and an HP LaserJetII. The terminfo database names these types 593ibm, 583eps, and 583hp, respectively. If you specify more than one printer type, the LP print service will use one of them as appropriate for each print request.

◆ *Note*   If you specify more than one printer type, you must specify simple as the content type.

While you are not required to specify a printer type, we recommend that you do so; when a printer type is specified, better print services can be provided.

To specify a printer type, use the following command line:

    lpadmin -p *printer-name* -T *printer-type-list*

If you give a list of printer types, separate the names with commas. If you do not define a printer type, the default unknown will be used.

❑ Listing the Content Types

While the printer type tells the LP print service what types of printers are being added, the content types tell the LP print service what types of files can be printed directly on each printer. Most printers can print files of two types: the same type as the printer type (if the printer type is defined) and the type `simple` (meaning an ASCII file), which is the default content type for all printers.

Some printers, though, can accept (and print properly) several different types of files. When adding this kind of printer, specify the names of the content types the new printer accepts by adding these names to the list. (By default, the list contains only one type: `simple`.) If you're adding a remote printer, list the content types that have been established for it by the administrator of the system on which it resides.

To specify the list of content types, enter the following command:

    lpadmin -p *printer-name* -I *content-type-list*

The *content-type-list* is a list of names separated by commas or spaces. If you use spaces to separate the names, enclose the entire list (but not the `-I`) in quotes.

Content type names may look a lot like printer type names, but you are free to choose names that are meaningful to you and the people using the printer. The names must contain no more than fourteen characters and may include only letters, digits, and underscores.

 ◆ *Note*   The names `simple` and `any` are meaningful to the LP print service; be sure to use them consistently. The name `terminfo` is also
reserved, as a reference to *all* types of printers.

Figure 3-2 lists and describes some accepted content types:

Figure 3-2: Common Content Types.
Content types describe the kind of files the printer can handle. These are the most common content types.

Content Type	Description
troff	Device independent output from troff
otroff	CAT typesetter instructions generated by BSD or pre-System V troff (old troff)
tex	DVI format files
plot	Plotting instructions for Tektronix displays and devices
raster	Raster bitmap format for Varian raster devices
cif	Output of BSD cifpbt
fortran	ASA carriage control format
postscript	PostScript language
simple	ASCII file

When a file is submitted to the LP print service for printing with the printer specified by the -d any option of the lp command, the print service searches for a printer capable of handling the job. The print service can identify an appropriate printer through either the content type name or the printer type name. Therefore, you may specify either name (or no name) when submitting a file for printing. If the same content type is printable by several different types of printers, you should use the same content type names when you add those printers. This makes it easier for the people using the printers, because they can use the same name to identify the type of file they want printed regardless of the printing destination.

Most manufacturers produce printers that accept simple ASCII files. While these printers are different types (and thus have different initialization control sequences), they may all be capable of handling the same type of file, which we call simple. As another example, several manufacturers may produce printers that accept ANSI X3.64 defined escape sequences. However, the printers may not support all the ANSI capabilities; they may support different sets of capabilities. You may want to differentiate them by assigning different content type names for these printers.

However, while it may be desirable (in situations such as these) to list content types for each printer, it is not always necessary to do so. If you don't, the printer type will be used as the name of the content type the printer can handle. If you have not specified a printer type, the LP print service will assume the printer can print only files of content type `simple`. This may be sufficient if you require users to specify the proper printer explicitly and if files are properly prepared for the printer before being submitted for printing.

The Default Content Type: `simple`

Files of content type `simple` are assumed to contain only two types of characters, printable ASCII characters and the control characters listed in Figure 3-3.

ASCII Code	Name	Action
0x08 010_8	backspace	Move the carriage back one space, except at the beginning of a line.
0x09 011_8	tab	Move the carriage to the next tab stop; by default, stops are spaced every 8 columns on most printers.
0x0a 012_8	linefeed	Move the carriage to the beginning of the next line. (This may require special port settings for some printers; see *Establishing Printer Port Characteristics* below.)
0x0c 014_8	formfeed	Move the carriage to the beginning of the next page.
0x0d 015_8	carriage return	Move the carriage to the beginning of the same line. (This may fail on some printers.)

Figure 3-3: ASCII Control Characters.
Files with content type simple can contain these control characters in addition to the printable characters. The control characters will be correctly interpreted on the printer and implement the indicated action.

The word "carriage" may be archaic for modern laser printers, but these printers do actions similar to those done by a carriage. If a printer can handle several types of files, including `simple`, you must include `simple` in the content type list; the type `simple` is not automatically added to any list you give. If you don't want a printer to accept files of type `simple`, give a blank *content-type-list*, as follows:

```
lpadmin -p printer-name -I ""
```

❑ Establishing Printer Port Characteristics

◆ *Note*   This section does not apply if you are making a remote printer available to users on your system.

Printers connected directly to computers and those connected over some networks require that the printer port characteristics be set by the interface program. These characteristics define the low level communications with the printer. Included are the baud rate; use of XON/XOFF flow control; 7, 8, or other bits per byte; type of parity; and output post-processing. The standard interface program will use the `stty` command to initialize the printer port, minimally setting the baud rate and a few other default characteristics. The default characteristics applied by the standard interface program are listed in Figure 3-4.

You may find that the default characteristics are sufficient for your printers. However, printers vary enough that you are likely to find that you have to set different characteristics. See the description of the `stty` command in the *UNIX System V Release 4 User's Reference Manual/System Administrator's Reference Manual* to find the complete list of characteristics.

If you have a printer that requires printer port characteristics other than those handled by the `stty` program, you will have to customize the interface program. See Chapter 5, *Customizing the Print Service*, for more information.

When you add a new printer, you may specify an additional list of port characteristics. The list you give will be applied after the default list, so that you do not need to include in your list items that you don't want to change. Specify the additional list as follows:

```
lpadmin -p printer-name -o "stty='stty-option-list'"
```

Note that both the double quotes and single quotes are needed if you give more than one item in the *stty-option-list*.

Default	Meaning
`9600`	9600 baud rate
`cs8`	8-bit bytes
`-cstopb`	1 stop bit per byte
`-parenb`	no parity generation
`ixon`	enable XON/XOFF flow control
`-ixany`	allow only XON to restart output
`opost`	post-process data stream as listed below:
`-olcuc`	don't map lower-case to upper-case
`onlcr`	map linefeed into carriage-return/linefeed
`-ocrnl`	don't map carriage-return into linefeed
`-onocr`	output carriage-returns even at column 0
`nl0`	no delay after linefeeds
`cr0`	no delay after carriage-returns
`tab0`	no delay after tabs
`bs0`	no delay after backspaces
`vt0`	no delay after vertical tabs
`ff0`	no delay after form-feeds

Figure 3-4:
Default `stty`
Options.
Here are the `stty`
*settings that will
be used if you
don't overide any
of them with the
* `-o` *option to*
`lpadmin`.

Example - Setting Printer Port Characteristics

Suppose your printer is to be used for printing graphical data, where linefeed characters should be output alone, without an added carriage-return. You would enter the following command:

```
lpadmin -p printer-name -o "stty=-onlcr"
```

Note that the single quotes are omitted when there's only one item in the list.

Example - Setting Printer Port Characteristics

Suppose your printer requires odd parity for data sent to it. You must turn on parity generation and detection (`parenb`), choose odd rather than even parity (`parodd`), and change the character size from 8 to 7 bits (`cs7`). Use the following command:

```
lpadmin -p printer-name -o "stty='parenb parodd cs7'"
```

❏ Listing Available Character Sets or Print Wheels

◆ *Note*   Although your users may use character sets or print wheels that have been mounted on a remote printer (by the administrator of the remote system on which that printer resides), you cannot mount a character set or a print wheel on a remote printer.

Printers differ in the way they can print different font styles. Some have changeable print wheels, some have changeable font cartridges, others have preprogrammed, selectable character sets.

When adding a printer, you may specify what print wheels, font cartridges, or character sets are available with the printer.

◆ *Note*   If you're adding a remote printer and you want your users to be able to use character sets or print wheels that have been mounted by the administrator of the remote system, you must list those character sets and print wheels, just as you would list the character sets and print wheels on a local printer.

Only one of these is assumed to apply to each printer. From the point of view of the LP print service, however, print wheels and changeable font cartridges are the same because they require you to intervene and mount a new print wheel or font cartridge. Thus, for ease of discussion, only print wheels and character sets will be mentioned.

When you list the print wheels or character sets available, you will be assigning names to them. These names are for your convenience and the convenience of the users. Because different printers may have similar print wheels or character sets, you should use common names for all printers. This allows a user to submit a file for printing and ask for a particular font style, without regard for which printer will be used or whether a print wheel or selectable character set is used.

If the printer has mountable print wheels, you need only list their names. If the printer has selectable character sets, you need to list their names and map each one into a name or number that uniquely identifies it in the `terminfo` database. Use the following command to determine the names of the character sets listed in the `terminfo` database:

```
tput -T printer-type csnm 0
```

where *printer-type* is the name of the printer type in question. The name of the 0th character set (the character set obtained by default after the printer is initialized) will be printed. Repeat the command, using 1, 2, 3, and so on in place of the 0, to see the names of the other character sets. In general, the `terminfo` names should closely match the names used in the user documentation for the printer. However, because not all manufacturers use the same names, the `terminfo` names may differ from one printer type to the next.

◆ *Note*   For the LP print service to be able to find the names in the `terminfo` database, you must specify a printer type. See the section *Setting the Printer Type* above.

To specify a list of print wheel names when adding a printer, enter the following command.

```
lpadmin -p printer-name -S print-wheel-list
```

The *print-wheel-list* is a comma or space separated list of names. If you use spaces to separate the names, enclose the entire list (but not the -S) in quotes. Both forms are shown below:

```
lpadmin -p diablo -S script,courier
lpadmin -p daisy -S "cyrillic symbol"
```

To specify a list of character set names and to map them into `terminfo` names or numbers, enter the following command:

```
lpadmin -p printer-name -S character-set-list
```

The *character-set-list* is also a comma or space separated list; however, each item in the list looks like one of the following:

cs*N*=*character-set-name*
character-set-name₁=*character-set-name₂*

In the first case, *N* is a number from 0 to 63 that identifies the number of the character set in the `terminfo` database. In the second case, *character-set-name₁* identifies the character set by its `terminfo` name. In either case the name to the right of the equal sign (=) is the name you may use as an alias for the character set.

◆ *Note*   You do not have to provide a list of aliases for the character sets if the `terminfo` names are adequate. You may refer to a character set by number, by `terminfo` name, or by your alias.

Example - Defining Character Sets

Suppose your printer has two selectable character sets (sets #1 and #2) in addition to the standard character set (set #0), and that the printer type is `5310`. To determine the names of the selectable character sets, enter the following `tput` commands (system output in response to the commands is shown in bold):

```
tput -T 5310 csnm 1
english
tput -T 5310 csnm 2
finnish
```

The words `english` and `finnish`, the output of the commands, are the names of the selectable character sets. You decide that the name `finnish` is adequate for referring to character set #2, but better names are needed for the standard set (set #0) and set #1. Enter the following command to define synonyms:

```
lpadmin -p·printer-name -S "cs0=american, english=british"
```

The following three commands will then produce identical results.

```
lp -S cs1 -d any ...
lp -S english -d any ...
lp -S british -d any ...
```

If you do not list the print wheels or character sets that can be used with a printer, then the LP print service will assume the following: a printer that takes print wheels has only a single, fixed print wheel, and users may not ask for a special print wheel when using the printer; and a printer that has selectable character sets can take any csN name or `terminfo` name known for the printer.

❏ Alerting to Mount a Print Wheel

◆ *Note*   This section does not apply if you are making a remote printer available to users on your system.

If you have printers that can take changeable print wheels, and have listed the print wheels allowed on each, then users will be able to submit a print request to use a particular print wheel. Until it is mounted though (see *Mounting a Form or Print Wheel* in Chapter 6, *Administering the LP Print Service*), a request for a print wheel will stay queued and will not be printed. You could periodically monitor the number of print requests pending for a particular print wheel, but the LP print service provides an easier way: you can ask to be alerted when the number of requests waiting for a print wheel has exceeded a specified threshold.

You can choose one of several ways to receive an alert.

▲   You can receive an alert via electronic mail.

▲   You can receive an alert written to any terminal on which you are logged in with `write`(1).

▲   You can receive an alert through a program of your choice.

▲   You can receive no alerts.

◆ *Note*   If you elect to receive no alerts, you are responsible for checking to
                see whether any print requests haven't printed because the proper
                print wheel isn't mounted.

In addition to the method of alerting, you can also set the number of requests
that must be queued before you are alerted, and you can arrange for repeated
alerts every few minutes until the print wheel is mounted. You can choose the
rate of repeated alerts, or you can opt to receive only one alert for each print
wheel.

To arrange for alerting to the need to mount a print wheel, enter one of the
following commands:

```
lpadmin -S print-wheel-name -A mail -Q requests -W minutes
lpadmin -S print-wheel-name -A write -Q requests -W minutes
lpadmin -S print-wheel-name -A 'command' -Q requests -W minutes
lpadmin -S print-wheel-name -A none
```

The first two commands direct the LP print service to send you a mail message or write the message directly to your terminal, respectively, for each
alert. The third command directs the LP print service to run the *command* for
each alert. The shell environment currently in effect when you enter the third
command is saved and restored for the execution of *command;* this includes
the environment variables, user and group IDs, and current directory. The
fourth command directs the print service to never issue an alert when a print
wheel needs to be mounted. The argument *requests* is the number of requests
that need to be waiting for the print wheel before the alert is triggered, and
the argument *minutes* is the number of minutes between repeated alerts.

◆ *Note*   If you want printer alerts sent to another user, use the third com-
                mand with the option -A 'mail *user-name*' or
                -A 'write *user-name*'. If you do not specify a *user-name*, the mail
                or message will be sent to your current ID. This may not be your
                login ID, if you have used the su command to change IDs.

When you start receiving repeated alerts, you can direct the LP print service
to stop sending you alerts for the current case by executing the following
command:

```
lpadmin -S print-wheel-name -A quiet
```

Once the print wheel has been mounted and unmounted again, alerts will
start again if too many requests are waiting. Alerts will also start again if the
number of requests waiting falls below the -Q threshold and then rises up to
the -Q threshold again, as when waiting requests are canceled, or if the type
of alerting is changed.

If *print-wheel-name* is all in any of the commands above, the alerting condition will apply to all print wheels for which an alert has already been defined.

If you don't define an alert method for a print wheel, you will not receive an
alert to mount it. If you do define a method without the -W option, you will
be alerted once for each occasion.

❑ Catching Printer Fault Alerts

◆ *Note*   This section does not apply if you are making a remote printer
                 accessible to users on your system.

The LP print service provides a framework for detecting printer faults and
alerting you to them. Faults can range from simple problems, such as running
out of paper or ribbon, or needing to replace the toner, to more serious faults,
such as a local power failure or a printer failure. The range of fault indicators
is also broad, ranging from dropping carrier (the signal that indicates that the
printer is on line), to sending an XOFF, to sending a message. Only two
classes of printer fault indicators are recognized by the LP print service itself:
a drop in carrier and an XOFF not followed in reasonable time by an XON.
However, you can add filters that recognize any other printer fault indicators,
and rely on the LP print service to alert you to a fault when the filter detects
it.

◆ *Note*   For a description of fault handling in filters, see Chapter 9, *Filters*.

You can choose one of several ways to receive an alert to a printer fault:

▲ You can receive an alert via electronic mail.

▲ You can receive an alert written to any terminal on which you are logged in.

▲ You can receive an alert through a program of your choice.

▲ You can receive no alerts.

◆ *Note*   If you elect to receive no alerts, you will need a way of finding out about the faults and fixing them; the LP print service will not continue to use a printer that has a fault.

In addition to the method of alerting, you can also arrange for repeated alerts every few minutes until the fault is cleared. You can choose the rate of repeated alerts, or you can choose to receive only one alert per fault.

Without a filter that provides better fault detection, the LP print service cannot automatically determine when a fault has been cleared except by trying to print another file. It will assume that a fault has been cleared when it is successfully able to print a file. Until that time, if you have asked for only one alert per fault, you will not receive another alert. If, after you have fixed a fault, but before the LP print service has tried printing another file, the printer faults again, or if your attempt to fix the fault fails, you will not be notified. Receiving repeated alerts per fault, or requiring manual re-enabling of the printer (see *Defining Printer Fault Recovery,* below), will overcome this problem.

To arrange for alerting to a printer fault, enter one of the following commands:

```
lpadmin -p printer-name -A mail -W minutes

lpadmin -p printer-name -A write -W minutes

lpadmin -p printer-name -A 'command' -W minutes

lpadmin -p printer-name -A none
```

The first two commands direct the LP print service to send you a mail message or write the message directly to your terminal, respectively, for each alert. The third command directs the LP print service to run the *command* for each alert. The shell environment currently in effect when you enter the third command is saved and restored for the execution of *command*. The environment includes environment variables, user and group IDs, and current directory. The fourth command directs the LP print service to never issue an alert when a fault occurs. The *minutes* argument is the number of minutes between repeated alerts.

◆ *Note*   If you want mail sent or a message written to another user when a printer fault occurs, use the third command with the option `-A 'mail` *user-name*`'` or `-A 'write` *user-name*`'`. If you do not specify a *user-name*, the mail or message will be sent to your current ID. This may not be your login ID, if you have used the `su` command to change IDs.

Once a fault occurs and you start receiving repeated alerts, you can direct the LP print service to stop sending you alerts (for the current fault only), by executing the following command:

```
lpadmin -p printer-name -A quiet
```

◆ *Note*   Use the alert type `quiet` only to terminate an active alert; do not specify `quiet` as the alert type for a new printer.

If the *printer-name* is `all` in any of the commands above, the alerting condition will apply to all printers.

If you don't define an alert method, you will receive mail once for each printer fault. If you define a method without the `-W` option, you will be alerted once for each fault.

❏ Defining Printer Fault Recovery

◆ *Note*   This section does not apply if you are making a remote printer
              accessible to users on your system.

When a printer fault has been fixed and the printer is ready for printing again,
the LP print service will recover in one of three ways:

   ▲   it will continue printing at the top of the page where printing stopped

   ▲   it will restart printing at the beginning of the print request that was
       active when the fault occurred

   ▲   it will wait for you to tell the LP print service to re-enable the printer

◆ *Note*   The ability to continue printing at the top of the page where printing
              stopped requires the use of a filter that can wait for a printer fault to
              be cleared before resuming properly. Such a filter probably has to
              have detailed knowledge of the control sequences used by the
              printer so it can keep track of page boundaries and know where in a
              file printing stopped. The default filter used by the LP print service
              cannot do this. If a proper filter is not being used, you will be noti-
              fied in an alert if recovery cannot proceed as you want.

To specify the way the LP print service should recover after a fault has been
cleared, enter one of the following commands:

```
lpadmin -p printer-name -F continue
lpadmin -p printer-name -F beginning
lpadmin -p printer-name -F wait
```

These commands direct the LP print service, respectively, to continue at the
top of the page, restart from the beginning, or wait for you to enter an
enable command to re-enable the printer (see the *Enabling and Disabling
Printers* section in this chapter for information on the enable command).

If you do not specify how the LP print service is to resume after a printer
fault, it will try to continue at the top of the page where printing stopped, or,
failing that, at the beginning of the print request.

If the recovery is `continue`, but the interface program does not stay running so that it can detect when the printer fault has been cleared, printing will be attempted every few minutes until it succeeds. You can force the LP print service to retry immediately by issuing an `enable` command.

❏ Adding a Printer Description

An easy way to give users of the LP print service helpful information about a printer is by adding a description of it. This description can contain any message you'd like, including the number of the room where the printer is found, the name of the person to call with printer problems, and so forth.

Users can see the message when they use the following command.

```
lpstat -D -p printer-name
```

To add a description of a printer, enter the following command.

```
lpadmin -p printer-name -D 'text'
```

The *text* is the message. You'll need to include the quotes if the message contains blanks or other characters that the shell might interpret if the quotes are left out.

❏ Setting Default Printing Attributes

When a user submits a print request, the page size, print spacing (character pitch and line pitch), and `stty` options are normally determined from the form that it will be printed on. When a user submits a print request without requesting a form, the print service uses one of several sets of default attributes.

- ▲ If the user has specified attributes to be used, those attributes will take precedence.

- ▲ If the user has not specified attributes, but the administrator has executed the `lpadmin -o` command option to set specific printing attributes for the printer, those attributes will take precedence.

▲ If neither of the above, the attributes defined in the `terminfo` database for the printer being used will take precedence.

The LP print service lets you override the defaults for each printer. Doing so can make it easier to submit print requests by allowing you to designate different printers as having different default page sizes or print spacing. A user can then simply route a file to the appropriate printer to get a desired style of output. For example, you can have one printer dedicated to printing wide (132-column) output, another printing normal (80-column by 66-line) output, and yet another printing letter quality (12 characters per inch, 8 lines per inch) output.

You can independently specify four default settings, page width, page length, character pitch, and line pitch. You can scale these to fit your needs: The first two can be given in characters and lines, or inches or centimeters. The last two can be given as characters and lines per inch or per centimeter. In addition, the character pitch can be specified as `pica` for 10 characters per inch (cpi), `elite` for 12 cpi, or `compressed` for the maximum cpi the printer can provide (up to a limit of 30 cpi).

Set the defaults using one or more of the following commands:

```
lpadmin -p printer-name -o width=scaled-number
lpadmin -p printer-name -o length=scaled-number
lpadmin -p printer-name -o cpi=scaled-number
lpadmin -p printer-name -o lpi=scaled-number
```

Append the letter `i` to the *scaled-number* to indicate inches, or the letter `c` to indicate centimeters. The letter `i` for character pitch (`cpi`) or line pitch (`lpi`) is redundant. You can also give `pica`, `elite`, or `compressed` instead of a number for the character pitch.

If you don't provide defaults when you configure a printer, then the page size and print spacing will be taken from the data for your printer type in the `terminfo` database. (If you do not specify a printer type, then the type will be `unknown`, for which there is an entry in the `terminfo` database.) You can find out what the defaults will be by first defining the printer configuration without providing your own defaults, then using the `lpstat` command to display the printer configuration. The command

```
lpstat  -p printer-name -l
```

will report the default page size and print spacing.

❑ Grouping Printers into Classes

◆ *Note*   This section does not apply if you are making a remote printer
accessible to users on your system.

A group of printers can be defined to constitute a single, named *class*. When
users submit a file for printing by a class, LP picks the first printer in the class
that it finds free. This allows faster turn-around, as printers are kept as busy
as possible.

Classes aren't needed if the only purpose is to allow a user to submit a print
request by type of printer. The lp -T content-type command (see *Listing the
Content Types* earlier in this chapter) allows a user to submit a file and specify
its type. The first available printer that can handle the type of the file will be
used to print it. The LP print service will avoid using a filter, if possible, by
choosing a printer that can print the file directly over one that would need it
filtered first.

◆ *Note*   See Chapter 9, *Filters* section of this chapter for more information
about filters.

Classes are used to establish a priority ordering of equivalent printers. For
example, group a high-speed printer and a low-speed printer in a single class;
the high-speed printer handles as many requests as possible and the low-
speed printer is reserved for use when the other is busy. This keeps both
printers as busy as possible.

You must add each printer to the system before adding it to a class, as
describing in an earlier section, *Establishing a Printer Name*. Classes are created, class membership is established and modified, and classes are deleted
with the lpadmin command.

Use the following command to add a printer to a class:

```
lpadmin -p printer-name -c class-name
```

If the class *class-name* doesn't exist yet, it will be created. The class name may contain a maximum of fourteen alphanumeric characters and underscores.

◆ *Note*   Class names and printer names must be unique. Because they are, a
              user can specify the destination for a print request without having
              to know whether it's a class of printers or a single printer.

You can remove a printer or class if it has no pending print requests. If there are pending requests, you have to first move them to another printer or class (using the `lpmove` command), or cancel them (using the `cancel` command). See Chapter 6, *Administering the Print Service*, and Chapter 7, *Managing the Print Load*.

Removing the last remaining printer of a class automatically removes the class as well. The removal of a class, however, does not cause the removal of printers that were members of the class. If the printer or class removed is also the system default destination, the system will no longer have a default destination.

To remove a printer or class, enter the following command:

```
lpadmin -x printer-or-class-name
```

If all you want to do is to remove a printer from a class without deleting that printer, enter the following command:

```
lpadmin -p printer-name -r class-name
```

❏ Defining the Interface Program

◆ *Note*   This section does not apply if you are making a remote printer
accessible to users on your system.

This is the program the LP print service uses to manage the printer each time
a file is printed. It has several tasks:

▲ to initialize the printer port (the connection between the computer
    and the printer)

▲ to initialize the printer (restore it to a normal state in case a previous
    print job left it in an unusual state) and set the character and line
    pitch, page size, and character set requested by the user

▲ to print a banner page

▲ to run a filter that prepares the file for printing

▲ to manage printer faults

If you do not choose an interface program, the standard one provided with
the LP print service will be used. This should be sufficient for most of your
printing needs. If you prefer, however, you can change it to suit your needs,
or completely rewrite your own interface program, and then specify it when
you add a new printer. See Chapter 5, *Customizing the Print Service,* for details
on how to customize an interface program.

If you are using the standard interface program, you needn't specify it when
adding a printer. If, however, you will be using a different interface program
on a local printer, you can refer to it either by specifying its full pathname or
by referring to another printer using the same interface program.

To identify a customized interface program by name, specify the printer
name and the pathname of the interface program, as follows:

```
lpadmin -p printer-name -i pathname
```

To use a customized interface program of another printer, specify the printer names as follows:

```
lpadmin -p printer-name₁  -e printer-name₂
```

where *printer-name$_1$* is the name of the printer you are adding and *printer-name$_2$* is the name of an existing printer that is using the customized interface program.

❏ Establishing User Access Restrictions

You can limit access to a given printer to a subset of users on your system. You may consider this option if one printer is reserved for printing sensitive information like checks, personnel evaluations, or financial reports. Or perhaps you have a printer that produces high quality but expensive output.

The LP print service will use a list of users allowed or denied access to a printer, and it will reject a user's request to print a file on a printer he or she is not allowed to use.

◆ *Note*   If your users have access to remote printers, or if users on other systems have access to printers on your system, make sure that the allow and deny lists for those printers on your computer match the allow and deny lists on the remote system where the remote printers reside. If these two sets of lists don't match, your users may receive conflicting messages (some accepting jobs and others refusing jobs) when submitting requests to remote printers.

The method of listing the users allowed or denied access to a printer is similar to the method used to list users allowed or denied access to the `cron` and `at` facilities, and the method described in Chapter 8 for allowing selective access to pre-printed forms. Briefly, the rules are as follows:

▲ An *allow list* is a list of users allowed to use the printer. A *deny list* is a list of users denied access to the printer.

▲ If the allow list is not empty, only the users listed are allowed; the deny list is ignored. If the allow list is empty, users listed in the deny list are not allowed. If both lists are empty, there are no restrictions on who may use the printer.

▲ Specifying `all` in the allow list allows everybody access to the printer; specifying `all` in the deny list denies access to everybody except the user `lp` and the superuser `root`.

You can add names of users to either list using one of the following commands:

```
lpadmin -p printer-name -u allow:user-list
lpadmin -p printer-name -u deny:user-list
```

where *user-list* is a list of names of users separated by a space or comma. The first command shown above adds the names to the allow list and removes them from the deny list. The second command adds the names to the deny list and removes them from the allow list. If you use spaces to separate the names, enclose the entire list (including the `allow:` or `deny:` but not the `-u`) in quotes. Each item in the *user-list* may take any of the forms shown in Figure 3-5.

If you do not provide allow and deny lists, the LP print service will assume that everybody may use the printer.

User-list Item	Meaning
user	*user* on any system
`all`	all users on all systems
local-system ! *user*	*user* on *local-system* only
! *user*	*user* on local system only
`all`!*user*	*user* on any system
`all`!`all`	all users on all systems
system!`all`	all users on *system*
`!all`	all users on local system

Figure 3-5: Limiting User Access to Printers.
The allow and deny lists contain entries of the form shown in the first column.

❏ Including a Banner Page in the Output

Most print requests should be preceded by a banner page. A banner page shows who requested the printing, the request ID for it, and when the output was printed. It also allows for an optional title that the requester can use to better identify a printout. Finally, the banner page greatly eases the task of separating a sequence of print requests so that each may be given to the correct user.

Sometimes a user needs to avoid printing a banner page. The likely occasions are when the printer has forms mounted that should not be wasted, such as payroll checks or accounts payable checks. Printing a banner page under such circumstances may cause problems.

Enter the following command to allow users to request no banner page:

```
lpadmin -p printer-name -o nobanner
```

If you later change your mind, you can reverse this choice by entering the following command:

```
lpadmin -p printer-name -o banner
```

If you do not allow a user to skip the banner page, the LP print service will reject all attempts to avoid printing a banner page. This is the default action.

❏ Putting It All Together

It is possible to add a new printer by completing a number of separate steps, shown in the commands described above. You may find it easier, however, to enter one or two commands that combine all the necessary arguments. Below are some examples.

Example - Adding a Local Printer

Add a new printer called `printer1` (of the type 455) on printer port `/dev/term/13`. It should use the standard interface program, with the default page size of 90 columns by 71 lines, and linefeeds should *not* be mapped into carriage return/linefeed pairs.

```
lpadmin -p printer1 -v /dev/term/13 -T 455 \
    -o "width=90 length=71 stty=-onlcr"
```

(The preceding command line is split into two lines for readability.)

Example- Using a Custom Interface Program

Add a new printer called `laser` on printer port `/dev/term/41`. It should use a customized interface program, located in the directory `/usr/doceng/laser_intface`. It can handle three file types (`i10`, `i300`, and `impress`) and it may be used only by the users `doceng` and `docpub`.

```
lpadmin -p laser -v /dev/term/41 \
    -i /usr/doceng/laser_intface \
    -I "i10,i300,impress" -u "allow:doceng,docpub"
```

(The preceding command line is split into three lines for readability.)

Example- Adding Printer Fault Alerts

When you added the `printer1` printer in the first example, you did not set the alerting. Do this now: have the LP print service alert you (by writing to the terminal on which you are logged in) every 10 minutes after a fault until you fix the problem.

```
lpadmin -p printer1 -A write -W 10
```

Example- Adding a Remote Printer

You can set up the printer service to print documents on a printer that is connected to another system. You must be able to communicate with the remote computer using TCP/IP, StarLAN, or some other Transport Interface-compatible network.

The following steps show you what to do on both your computer (the *client*) and the remote computer that services the remote printer (the *server*). The printer is a PostScript-compatible printer and the network is TCP/IP. The printer is able to print PostScript, `troff`, and `simple` documents.

Make sure you have TCP/IP installed and configured to communicate with the remote computer and confirm that the port monitor is able to accept print requests over the network by typing:

```
pmadm -l -p tcp
```

You see service tags for services 0 and `lp` associated with the network listener, in this case, `tcp`. See the *Network User's and Administrator's Guide* for information.

Identify the remote computer to the LP Print Service by typing:

```
lpsystem -t s5 -R 5 -T 10 dahlia
```

In this example, the options say that the system is running a System V scheduler (`-t s5`), that if a data transfer fails, retry every five minutes (`-R 5`), that if the connection is idle for 10 minutes, drop it (`-T 10`), and that the remote system of interest is called `dahlia`. See Chapter 2, *Installing the LP Print Service*, for more information about `lpsystem` and its options.

Identify the remote printer to the LP Print Service as follows:

```
lpadmin -p psjet -s dahlia!psjet1 \
   -I simple,troff,postscript
```

The local name for the printer is `psjet`; the printer's name on the remote system, `dahlia`, is `psjet1`. The `-I` option gives the acceptable content types.

To enable the printer and allow it to accept print jobs, type:

```
enable dahlia
accept dahlia
```

For this example, we assume that dahlia!psjet1 is properly configured and enabled on the server dahlia. Each client system must be defined in the server's `/etc/hosts` file and be identified to the server with the `lpsystem` command. If the local system is named `lily`, enter the following command on `dahlia`:

```
lpsystem -t s5 -R 5 -T 10 lily
```

This uses the same options that we established with `lpsystem` on our local system, `lily`.

❑ Examining a Printer Configuration

Once you've defined a printer configuration, you probably want to review it to see if it is correct. If after examining the configuration you find you've made a mistake, just reenter the command that applies to the part that's wrong.

Use the `lpstat` command to examine both the configuration and the current status of a printer. The short form of this command gives just the status; you can use it to see if the printer exists and if it is busy, idle, or disabled. The long form of the command gives a complete configuration listing.

Enter one of the following commands to examine a printer.

```
lpstat -p printer-name
lpstat -p printer-name -l
```

The second command is the long form. With either command you should see one of the following lines of output.

    printer *printer-name* now printing *request-id*. enabled since *date*.

    printer *printer-name* is idle. enabled since *date*.

    printer *printer-name* disabled since *date*.
            reason

    printer *printer-name* waiting for auto-retry.
            reason

The waiting for auto-retry output shows that the LP print service failed in trying to use the printer, because of the *reason* shown, and that it will try again later.

With the long form of the command, you should also see the following output:

    Form Mounted: *form-name*
    Content types: *content-type-list*
    Printer type: *printer-type*
    Description: *comment*
    Connection: *connection-info*
    Interface: *pathname*
    On fault: *alert-method*
    After fault: *fault-recovery*
    Users allowed
    user-list
    Forms allowed:
    form-list
    Banner required
    Character set:
    character-set-list
    Default pitch: *integer* CPI, *integer* LPI
    Default page size:
        scaled-decimal-number wide, *scaled-decimal-number* long
    Default port settings: *stty-option-list*

Each print request is sent to a "spooling daemon" that keeps track of all requests. The daemon is created when you start the LP print service. This UNIX system process is also responsible for keeping track of the status of printers and slow filters; when a printer finishes printing a user's file, the daemon starts it printing another request (if there is one queued).

❏ Accepting Print Requests for a New Printer

There are two steps in making a printer ready for use after you've defined the printer configuration. First, you must instruct the LP print service to accept print requests for the new printer. Second, you must activate or enable the new printer. These tasks are separate steps because you may have occasion to want to do one but not the other.

Initially, the LP print service will not consider a new printer eligible for printing files. This gives you time to make sure you've defined the printer configuration the way you want it. When you are ready to make the printer available, use `accept` to tell the LP print service to begin accepting print requests for it.

    `accept` *printer-or-class-name*

To prevent the print service from accepting any more requests, execute the following command.

    `reject` *printer-or-class-name*

These commands are described in more detail in Chapter 6, *Administering the LP Print Service*.

❏ Enabling and Disabling a Printer

When a printer is ready for use and the LP print service is accepting print requests for it, you must enable it before anything will print. This gives you time to verify that the correct form is loaded in your printer, the correct print wheel or font cartridge is in place, and the printer is on-line. When everything is ready, issue the `enable` command for the printer, as follows:

```
enable printer-name
```

If you want to enable several printers simultaneously, list the printers (separating the names with spaces) on the same line as the `enable` command. Don't enclose the list in quotes.

Disabling a printer stops further print requests from being printed. (It does not, however, stop the LP print service from accepting new print requests for the printer.) From time to time you may want to disable a printer. For example, you may want to interrupt a print request, or you may want to change a form or print wheel, in which case you should disable the printer first. Normally, disabling a printer also stops the request that's currently being printed, placing it back in the queue so it can be printed later. You can, however, have the LP print service wait until the current request finishes, or even cancel the request outright.

To disable a printer, enter one of the following commands:

```
disable -r "reason" printer-name

disable -W -r "reason" printer-name

disable -c -r "reason" printer-name
```

The first command disables the printer, stopping the currently printing request and saving it for printing later. The other commands also disable the printer, but the second one makes the LP print service wait for the current request to finish, while the third cancels the current request. The *reason* is stored and displayed whenever anyone checks the status of the printer. You can omit it (and the `-r` option) if you don't want to specify a reason.

◆ *Note*   The `-c` and `-W` options are not valid when the disable command is run to stop a remote printer because, when run for a remote printer, disable stops the transferring (rather than the actual printing) of print requests.

Several printers can be disabled at once by listing their names in the same line as the `disable` command.

Note   You can only enable or disable local printers; the loading of forms, print wheels, and cartridges in a remote printer and the enabling of that printer are the responsibility of the administrator of the remote system. You can, however, enable or disable the transfer of print requests to the remote system on which a printer is located. Only individual printers can be enabled and disabled; classes cannot.

Allowing Users to Enable and Disable a Printer

You may want to make the `enable` and `disable` commands available for use by other users. This is useful, for instance, if you have a small organization where anyone who spots a problem with the printer should be able to disable it and fix the problem. This is *not* a good idea if you want to keep others from interfering with the proper operation of the print services.

If you want to allow others to use the `enable` and `disable` commands, use a standard UNIX system feature called the "setuid bit." By assigning ownership of these commands to the user `lp` (this should have been done automatically when you installed the software), and by setting the setuid bit, anyone will be allowed to use the `enable` and `disable` commands. Clearing the bit removes this privilege.

To allow everybody to run `enable` and `disable`, enter the following two commands as user `lp` or superuser `root`:

```
chown lp /usr/bin/enable /usr/bin/disable
chmod u+s /usr/bin/enable /usr/bin/disable
```

The first command makes the user `lp` the owner of the commands; this step should be redundant, but it is safer to run the command than to skip it. The second command turns on the setuid bit.

To prevent others from running `enable` and `disable`, enter the following command as the super user `root`:

```
chmod u-s /usr/bin/enable /usr/bin/disable
```

❑ More About `lpadmin`

The `lpadmin` command has been used in many ways in this chapter to con-figure printers. This section presents all the options and uses of `lpadmin` in one place. Use it as a reference when you need to look up the details of a par-ticular option.

`lpadmin` configures the LP print service by defining printers and devices. It is used to add and change printers, to remove printers from the service, to set or change the system default destination, to define alerts for printer faults, and to mount print wheels.

Several forms of the command are accepted:

    lpadmin -p *printer options*

    lpadmin -x *dest*

    lpadmin -d [*dest*]

    lpadmin -S *print-wheel* -A *alert-type* [-W *minutes*] [-Q *requests*]

The first form of the command is used to configure a new printer or to change the configuration of an existing printer. The second form is used to remove a printer or a class from the LP print service. The third form sets a system default destination printer, and the fourth form defines the alerting method when print wheels need to be mounted. Figure 3-6 summarizes the options.

Option	Description
-A *alert-type* [-W *minutes*]	Define an alert to inform the administrator when a printer fault is detected, and periodically thereafter, until the printer fault is cleared by the administrator.
	alert-type is defined below, in Figure 3-7.
	If the *printer* is all, the *alert-type* applies to all existing printers.
	If the -W option is not used to arrange fault alerting for *printer*, the default procedure is to mail one message to the administrator of *printer* per fault. This is equivalent to specifying -W once or -W 0. If *minutes* is a number greater than zero, an alert will be sent every *minutes*.
-c *class*	Insert *printer* into *class*. The *class* is created if necessary.
-D *comment*	Display *comment* whenever a user asks for a description of *printer* with the lpstat command.
-d *printer-or-class-name*	Make *printer-or-class-name* the new system default destination.
	No other options are allowed with -d.
-e *printer2*	Use *printer2*'s interface program for *printer*. Options -i and -m may not be specified with -e.
-F *fault-recovery*	Specify the recovery action after a printer fault. Values for *fault-recovery* are presented in Figure 3-8.
-f allow:*form-list* -f deny:*form-list*	Allow or deny the forms in *form-list* to be printed on *printer*. By default no forms are allowed on a new printer. See Chapter 8, *Preprinted Forms* and the *Forms Access* section below for more information on constructing a *form-list*. Note the other use of -f, with the -M option.
-h	*printer* is hardwired. -h and -l are mutually exclusive options; -h is the default.

Figure 3-6: lpadmin Options. Use these options to configure printers for the LP Print Service.

Option	Description
-I *content-type-list*	Allow *printer* to handle print requests with the content types listed in *content-type-list*. If the list includes more than one type, the names must be separated by commas or blank spaces. If they are separated by blank spaces, the entire list must be enclosed in double quotes.
	The type simple is the default content type. A simple file is a data stream containing only printable ASCII characters and the control characters listed in Figure 3-3.
	To prevent the print service from considering simple a valid type for the printer, specify either an explicit value (such as the printer type) in the *content-type-list*, or an empty list. If you do want simple included along with other types, you must include simple in the *content-type-list*.
	Except for simple, each *content-type* name is freely determined by the administrator. If the printer type is specified by the -T option, then the printer type is implicitly considered to be a valid content type.
-i *interface*	Establish an interface program for *printer*. *interface* is the pathname. -e and -m cannot be specified with -i.
-l	*printer* is a login terminal. The LP scheduler (lpsched) disables all login terminals when it starts up. -h cannot be specified with -l.
-M -f *form* [-a [-o file-break]]	Mount *form* on *printer*. If the -a option is given, print an alignment pattern. If the -o filebreak option is given, a formfeed is inserted between each copy of the alignment pattern. See Chapter 8, *Pre-printed Forms*, for more details.

Option	Description
-M -S *print-wheel*	Mount *print-wheel* on *printer*. Print requests that need *print-wheel* will be printed on *printer*. If more than one printer has *print-wheel* mounted and the user has specified `any` (with the -d option of the `lp` command) as the printer destination, then the print request will be printed on the one printer that also meets the other needs of the request. If *print-wheel* is not listed as acceptable for *printer*, the administrator is warned but the mount is accepted. If the printer does not take print wheels, the command is rejected. A print wheel is dismounted either by mounting a new print wheel in its place or by using the option -S none. By default, a new printer has no print wheel mounted. Note the other uses of the -S option without the -M option described below.
-m *model*	Use the *model* interface program provided with the LP print service. -e and -i cannot be specified with -m.
-o *print-option=value*	*print-option* supplies a default given to an interface program if the *print-option* value is not taken from a preprinted form description or is not explicitly given by the user submitting a request. The possible *print-option*s are shown in Figure 3-9.
-o nobanner	Allow a user to submit a job specifying that no banner page be printed.
-o banner	Force a banner page to be printed with every print request, even when the user requests otherwise. This is the default.
-p *printer*	*printer* is the name of a printer.

Option	Description
-r *class*	Remove *printer* from *class*. Remove *class* if it is empty.
-S *list*	Allow the print wheels or character sets named in *list* to be used on *printer*. *list* is a comma or space separated list of print wheel or character set names. Enclose the list with quotes if it contains blanks.
	For printers that take print wheels: *list* will be the only print wheels considered mountable on the printer, although the administrator can always force a different print wheel to be mounted. Until a *list* is specified, no print wheels will be considered mountable on the printer, and print requests that ask for a particular print wheel with this printer will be rejected.
	For printers with selectable character sets: Each item in *list* maps a character set name to an alias and is of the form *known-name=alias*. *where known-name* is a character set number preceded by cs (*e.g.* cs3 for character set three) or a character set name from the terminfo database entry csnm. Until a *list* is specified, only the names already known from terminfo and numbers with a prefix of cs will be recognized.
	If *list* is none, any existing print wheel lists or character set aliases will be removed.
	Note the other uses of the -S with the -M option described above, and with the -A switch described below.
-S *print-wheel* -A *alert-type* [-W *minutes*] [-Q *requests*]	Define an alert to be sent when a print wheel needs to be mounted. *alert-type* and *minutes* are described under the -A option. *requests* is the number of print requests that must be queued before the alert is sent.
	If *print-wheel* is all, the alerting defined here applies to all print wheels. Not specifying -Q is equivalent to -Q 1 or -Q any, and is the default.

Option	Description
-s *systemname* [! *printer-name*]	Make the remote printer *printer-name* on *system-name* accessible to users on your system as *printer*. *system-name* must be listed in the systems table (`/etc/lp/Systems`). *printer-name* is the name used on the remote system for that printer, and may differ from *printer*.
-T *printer-type-list*	Identify the printer as being of one or more *printer-type*s. Each *printer-type* is used to extract data from the `terminfo` database; this information is used to initialize the printer before printing each user's request. The default *printer-type* is `unknown` and no information is extracted from `terminfo`; each user request is printed without first initializing the printer. This option must be used if the following are to work: `-o cpi`, `-o lpi`, `-o width`, and `-o length` options of the `lpadmin` and `lp` commands, and the `-S` and `-f` options of the `lpadmin` command. If the *printer-type-list* contains more than one type, then the *content-type-list* of the `-I` option must either be specified as `simple`, as empty (`-I " "`), or not specified at all.
-u allow: *user-list* -u deny : *user-list*	Allow or deny the users in *user-list* access to the printer. By default all users are allowed on a new printer. The *user-list* may include any or all of the constructs shown in Figure 3-5. For each printer the LP print service keeps two lists of users: an *allow-list* of people allowed to use the printer, and a *deny-list* of people denied access to the printer. Users are added to *allow-list* and removed from *deny-list* with `-u allow`. Users are added to *deny-list* and removed from *allow-list* with `-u deny`. If *allow-list* is not empty, only the users in the list may use the printer, regardless of the contents of *deny-list*. If *allow-list* is empty, the users in *deny-list* may not use the printer. All users can be denied access to the printer by specifying `-u deny:all`. All users may use the printer by specifying `-u allow:all`.

Option	Description
-U *dial-info*	Assign the dialing information *dial-info* to the printer for use with the `dial` routine to call the printer. Any network connection supported by the Basic Network Utilities will work. *dial-info* can be either a phone number for a modem connection or a system name for other kinds of connections. Use -U `direct` for a printer that is directly connected. If a system name is given in *dial-info*, it is used to search for connection details from the file `/etc/u-ucp/Systems` or related files. The Basic Network Utilities are required to support this option. By default, -U `direct` is assumed.
-v *device*	Associate *device* with *printer*. *device* is the pathname of a file that is writable by `lp`, and can be associated with more than one printer.
-x *printer-or-class-name*	Remove *printer-or-class-name*. If an empty class remains, it will be deleted. If *printer-or-class-name* is `all`, all printers and classes are removed. No other options are allowed with -x.

Printer Alerts

The -A option specifies alert actions for conditions like requests to mount a different form, print wheel, or character set, or for printer fault conditions like paper jams, out of paper, out of toner, printer off-line, etc. The *alert-types* are shown in Figure 3-7.

The alert message sent when `mail` or `write` is chosen appears as follows:

```
The printer printer has stopped printing for the reason
given below. Fix the problem and bring the printer
back on line. Printing has stopped, but will be
restarted in a few minutes; issue an enable command if
you want to restart sooner. Unless someone issues a
change request

lp -i request-id -P …

to change the page list to print, the current request
will be reprinted from the beginning.

The reason(s) it stopped (multiple reasons indicate
reprinted attempts):
```

reason

The LP print service can detect printer faults only through an adequate fast
filter and only when the standard interface program or a suitable customized
interface program is used. Furthermore, the level of recovery after a fault
depends on the capabilities of the filter.

Value	Description
mail	Send the alert message via mail to the administrator.
write	Write the message to the terminal on which the administrator is logged in. If the administrator is logged in on several terminals, one is chosen arbitrarily.
quiet	Do not send messages for the current condition. An administrator can use this option to temporarily stop receiving further messages about a known problem. Once the fault has been cleared and printing resumes, messages will again be sent when another fault occurs with the printer.
none	Do not send messages; any existing alert definition for the printer will be removed. No alert will be sent when the printer faults until a different alert-type (except quiet) is used.

Figure 3-7: Possible Values for alert-type. You can specify what the print service will do when a printer fault or mount request occurs.

Value	Description
shell-com- mand	Run the shell-command each time the alert needs to be sent. The shell command should expect the message in standard input. If there are blanks embedded in the command, enclose the command in quotes. Note that the `mail` and `write` values for this option are equivalent to the values `mail` *user-name* and `write` *user-name* respectively, where *user-name* is the current name for the administrator. This will be the login name of the person submitting this command unless he or she has used the `su` command to change to another user ID. If the `su` command has been used to change the user ID, then the *user-name* for the new ID is used.
list	Display the type of the alert for the printer fault. No change is made to the alert.

Fault Recovery

The -F option specifies the recovery to be used for any print request that is stopped because of a printer fault, according to the value of *fault-recovery*:

Figure 3-8: Possible values for fault-recovery. You can specify the printer action after a printer fault is cleared.

Option	Description
continue	Continue printing on the top of the page where printing stopped. This requires a filter to wait for the fault to clear before automatically continuing.
beginning	Start printing the request again from the beginning.
wait	Disable printing on *printer* and wait for the administrator or a user to enable printing again.

During the wait the administrator or the user who submitted the stopped print request can issue a change request that specifies where printing should resume. If no change request is made before printing is enabled, printing will resume at the top of the page where stopped, if the filter allows; otherwise, the request will be printed from the beginning.

Forms Access

For each printer, the LP print service keeps two lists of forms: an *allow-list* of forms that may be used with the printer, and a *deny-list* of forms that may not. Forms listed are added to the *allow-list* and removed from the *deny-list* with the -f allow option. Forms are added to the *deny-list* and removed from the *allow-list* using the -f deny option.

If *allow-list* is not empty, only the forms in that list may be used on the printer, regardless of the contents of *deny-list*. If *allow-list* is empty, but *deny-list* is not, the forms in *deny-list* may not be used with the printer. All forms can be excluded from a printer by specifying -f deny:all. All forms can be used on a printer, provided the printer can handle all the characteristics of each form, by specifying -f allow:all.

The LP print service uses this information as a set of guidelines for determining where a form can be mounted. Administrators, however, are not restricted from mounting a form on any printer. If mounting a form on a particular printer disagrees with the information in *allow-list* or *deny-list*, the administrator is warned but the mount is accepted. Nonetheless, if a user attempts to issue a print or change request for a form and printer combination that is in disagreement with the information, the request is accepted only if the form is currently mounted on the printer. If the form is later unmounted before the request can print, the request is canceled and the user is notified by mail.

If the administrator tries to specify a form as acceptable for use on a printer that doesn't have the capabilities needed by the form, the command is rejected.

Printing Attributes

The -o option is used to define printing parameters like page size and character density. Figure 3-9 shows the acceptable values for *print-option* as well as the defaults for each one.

*Figure 3-9: Pos-
sible values for
print-option.*
*You can specify
printing parame-
ters like page
length and width
and character den-
sity, and commu-
nication parame-
ters controlled
with* stty.

Option	Meaning	Default
length=*scaled-decimal-number*	page length	Defined in the terminfo entry for the specified printer type.
		To set or reset to the default value, use length=
width=*scaled-decimal-number*	page width	Defined in the terminfo entry for the specified printer type.
		To set or reset to the default value, use width=
cpi=*scaled-decimal-number*	characters per inch	Defined in the terminfo entry for the specified printer type.
		To set or reset to the default value, use cpi=
lpi=*scaled-decimal-number*	lines per inch	Defined in the terminfo entry for the specified printer type.
		To set or reset to the default value, use lpi=
stty='*stty-option-list*'	stty parameters	stty='9600 cs8 -cstopb \ -parenb ixon -ixany opost \ -olcuc onlcr -ocrnl -onoc \ -onlret -ofill nl0 cr0 \ tab0 bs0 vt0 ff0'
		To set or reset to the default value, use stty=

The *scaled-decimal-number* is a non-negative number indicating a unit of size. The unit is shown by a trailing letter attached to the number: c for centime-ters, i for inches, and no letter for "appropriate" units, that is, lines, charac-ters, lines per inch, or characters per inch. The *scaled-decimal-number* must be consistent with the physical capabilities of physical printer, as defined in the terminfo database. Otherwise, the command is rejected.

The *stty-option-lis*t is not checked for allowed values, but is passed directly to the `stty` program by the standard interface program. Any error messages produced by `stty` when a request is processed by the standard interface program are mailed to the user submitting the request.

Restrictions

▲ When creating a new printer, one of three options (`-v`, `-U`, or `-s`) must be supplied.

▲ Only one of the following may be supplied: `-e`, `-i`, or `-m`. If none of these three options is supplied, the model standard is used.

▲ The `-h` and `-l` options are mutually exclusive.

▲ Printer and class names may be no longer than 14 characters and must consist entirely of the characters `A-Z`, `a-z`, `0-9` and `_` (underscore).

▲ If `-s` is specified, the following options are invalid: `-A`, `-e`, `-F`, `-h`, `-i`, `-l`, `-M`, `-m`, `-o`, `-U`, `-v`, and `-W`.

4

Using Menus to Configure Printers

❏ **Overview**

The previous chapter presented the shell commands that are used to configure printers for the LP print service. All of these tasks can be accomplished using the printer service menus, which are presented in this chapter.

Type `sysadm` and choose `printers` from the resulting menu to invoke the Printer Services menu, shown in Figure 4-1. Two entries in this menu are used to configure printers: `printers` and `classes`. This chapter will walk you through the same tasks as described in the previous chapter, defining

- ▲ *the required parameters*: printer name, device address (or connection method), and, for remote printers, the system name

- ▲ *the parameters that characterize the printer*: printer type, content types, printer port characteristics, available printwheels and character sets, alert methods and fault recovery, default printing attributes, and printer description

▲ *the parameters that characterize the print service for this printer*: printer classes, user access restrictions, banner pages, and interface program characteristics

Much of the descriptive material from Chapter 3 is repeated here, albeit with different words.

Figure 4-1: LP Printer Services Menu.
Choose print-ers *to add, remove, and configure printers.*

```
2  Line Printer Services Configuration and Operation
------------------------------------------------------
classes    - Manage Classes of Related Printers
filters    - Manage Filters for Special Processes
forms      - Manage Pre-printed Forms
operations- Perform Daily Printer Service Operations
printers   - Configure Printers for the Printer Service
priorities- Assign Print Queue Priorities to Users
requests   - Manage Active Print Requests
status     - Display Status of Printer Service
systems    - Configure Connection to Remote Systems
preSVR4    - Printer Setup
```

❏ Adding a Local Printer

Select the printer entry in the Printer Services menu (Figure 4-1) to invoke the menu for configuring printers, shown in Figure 4-2 with the add entry highlighted. Select add to produce a dialog box to enter the printer parameters, shown in Figure 4-3. Note that default values are already filled in, but can be overridden by replacing the defaults with values better suited to your printer.

```
3   Configure Printers for the Printer Service
-------------------------------------------------
add     - Add a New Printer
list    - Display Printer Configuration Information
modify  - Modify Printer Configuration
remove  - Remove Printer
```

Figure 4-2: Con figure Printers Menu.
Choose add to add new printers to the LP Print Service.

```
4   Add a New Printer
-------------------------------------------------
Printer name:
System name:
Printer type: unknown
Similar printer to use for defaults: none
Do you want to use standard configurations (e.g. alerts,
banners)? yes
Do you want to use standard port settings (e.g. baud rate,
parity)? yes
Device or Address:
```

Figure 4-3: Add a New Printer Dialog Box.
Fill in the blanks to add a new printer. the bold face type shows default values.

Only two fields are required when adding a local printer:

```
Printer name:
```

This field defines the name that users will use to direct output to this specific printer. The name can contain up to 14 characters.

```
Device or Address:
```

This field defines the connection method. When the printer is hard-wired, fill in this field with the device name for the port it is plugged in to (/dev/term/00, for example). If the printer is connected to a modem, this field would contain the phone number used to dial the modem. This field is blank if the printer is connected to a remote system.

The remaining fields in the `Add a New Printer` dialog box have default values that will be used if you don't override them.

```
( System name:                                                              )
```

The system name is the identification of the computer system to which the printer is attached. Remote systems must be registered with the Basic Network Services. If no system name is given, the local system name will be used

```
( Printer type:                                                             )
```

The default value is `unknown`. The printer type is used to extract terminfo(4) characteristics of the printer, describing the capabilities and control information. It is the generic name for the printer, and is typically derived from the manufacturer's name for the device.

```
( Similar printer to use for defaults:                                      )
```

The default value is `none`. If you have already added a printer that is similar to this one, you can use the defaults you set up for it by entering its name here.

```
( Do you want to use the standard configurations?                          )
```

The default is `yes`. If you choose `no`, you will see the dialog box shown in Figure 4-4. The default entries show the standard configuration.

```
( Class:                                                                    )
```

Add the printer to a class. See the discussion in *Adding a Printer to a Class* later in this chapter.

```
( Description:                                                              )
```

Add a description of the printer. It might include the location of the printer, the name of the person to call when there is a problem with the printer, and so on. You can see the message by typing:

```
lpstat -D -p printer-name
```

```
( File types printable without filtering: )
```

The default is simple, describing files that contain only ASCII characters and standard control characters (backspace, tab, linefeed, carriage return, or formfeed). When adding a printer that can accept other kinds of files without filtering, list the acceptable content types here.

```
( Can the user skip a banner page? )
```

The banner page shows you who requested the printing, the request ID, and when it was printed, and allows for an optional title that the submitter can use to help identify the output.

Sometimes a user needs to avoid printing a banner, like when the printer has expensive forms mounted. Type yes and override the default if you want the user to be able to omit the banner page.

```
Default character pitch:
Default line pitch:
Default page width:
Default page length:
```

Printing attributes are normally determined from a form specification, or from the default attributes specified here. You can independently specify page width, page length, character pitch, and line pitch. The first two can be given in columns and lines, inches, or centimeters. The last two can be specified as characters or lines per inch or per centimeter. In addition, the character pitch can be specified as pica (10 characters per inch, or 10 cpi), elite (12 cpi), or compressed (the maximum cpi the printer can provide, up to 30 cpi)

```
Command to run for alerts:
Frequency of alert (in minutes):
```

The print service provides a framework for detecting printer faults and alerting you when a fault occurs. You specify the command that will be run if a fault alert is required, and the frequency with which the alert will be given. The defaults are "mail lp" and once.

If you elect to receive no alerts, you will need a way of finding out about faults and fixing them; LP will not continue to use a printer that has a fault.

Without a filter that provides better fault detection, LP cannot automatically determine when a fault has been cleared except by trying to print another file. The print service will assume that a fault has been cleared when it is able to print a file. Until that time, if you have asked for only one alert per fault, you will not receive another alert. If the printer faults again after you have cleared the previous fault but before another file is printed, you will not be notified. Receiving repeated alerts per fault or requiring manual re-enabling of the printer will overcome this problem.

```
Printer recovery method:
```

You can enter continue, restart, or wait. The default is restart. The ability to continue printing at the top of the page where the fault occurred requires the use of a filter that can wait until the fault is cleared before resuming operation. Such a filter is both printer and content specific, and the default filter cannot provide this function.

```
Is the printer also a login terminal?
```

The default is no. Say yes if appropriate.

```
Do you want to use the standard port settings?
```

The default is yes. If you choose no, you will see the dialog box shown in Figure 4-5 that will lead you through the task of defining the low-level communication parameters for the printer. The standard interface program uses stty to initialize the printer port, setting the baud rate and a few other characteristics. The defaults are shown in bold face type in Figure 4-5.

If you have a printer that requires printer port characteristics that cannot be set with stty, you will have to customize the interface program (see the section called *Modifying the Interface Program* in Chapter 5).

```
5  Configure New Printer "id," Local Printer Subtask
---------------------------------------------------------
Printer:

Class: none
Description of the printer: none
File types printable without filtering: simple
Can a user skip a banner page: no
Default character pitch: Use printer defaults
Default line pitch: Use printer defaults
Default page width: Use printer defaults
Default page length: Use printer defaults
Command to run for alerts: "mail lp"
Frequency of alerts (in minutes): once
Printer recovery method: beginning
Is the printer also a login terminal? no
```

Figure 4-4: Printer Configuration Dialog Box. Fill in the blanks to define printer characteristics. Default values are shown in bold face type.

```
5  Printer Communication Setup Subtask
---------------------------------------------------------
Printer: id
Baud rate: 9600
Parity: none
Stop bits: 1
Character size: 8
Hangup on loss of carrier: yes
XON/XOFF output control: yes
Allow any character to restart output: no
Postprocess output: yes
Man NL to CR-NL on output: yes
Map lower case to upper case on output: no
Carriage return delay: none
Newline Delay: no
Backspace delay: no
Formfeed delay: no
Vertical Tab Delay: no
Horizontal Tab Delay: expand
Other options:
```

Figure 4-5: Printer Communication Setup Dialog Box. Fill in the blanks to characterize the communication channel between the printer and the LP Print Service. Default values are shown in bold face type.

Example- Adding a PostScript Printer

We want to add a hardwired PostScript-compatible printer. It is an Apple Laserwriter named `iris` and will be connected with an RS232-C cable and null modem to the first serial port, `/dev/term/00`, on our system.

1. Change the ownership of the device entry for your printer port to make it accessible only to lp:

    ```
    chown lp /dev/term/00
    chgrp bin /dev/term/00
    chmod 600 /dev/term/00
    ```

2. Go to the `Add a New Printer` dialog box (shown in Figure 4-3) by typing `sysadm` to the shell, then selecting `printers` from menu 1, `printers` from menu 2, and `add` from menu 3. Fill in the dialog box as shown in Figure 4-6.

3. Press `save`.

4. When the `Configure New Printer` dialog box appears, fill it in as shown in the bottom half of Figure 4-6. The two important entries are `PS`, to insure proper filtering, and `continue`, to let the filter handle printer fault recovery.

5. Press `save`.

6. Leave the `sysadm` interface and return to the shell.

7. To enable the printer and allow it to accept print requests, type

    ```
    enable iris
    accept iris
    ```

8. To confirm that the printer is working, print a file:

    ```
    lp -d iris .profile
    ```

```
4   Add a New Printer
------------------------------------------------
Printer name: iris
System name: rose
Printer type: PSR
Similar printer to use for defaults: none
Do you want to use standard configurations (e.g. alerts,
banners)? no
Do you want to use standard port settings (e.g. baud
rate, parity)? yes
Device or Address:/dev/term/00
```

```
5   Configure New Printer "iris", Local Printer Subtask
---------------------------------------------------------
Printer: iris

Class: none
Description of the printer: none
File types printable without filtering: PS
Can a user skip a banner page: no
Default character pitch: Use printer defaults
Default line pitch: Use printer defaults
Default page width: Use printer defaults
Default page length: Use printer defaults
Command to run for alerts: "mail lp"
Frequency of alerts (in minutes): once
Printer recovery method: continue
Is the printer also a login terminal? no
```

Figure 4-6: Example: Adding a Postscript Printer.
The printer type PSR and the content type PS identify this printer, iris, as a PostScript printer. The second screen is displayed whenever you elect to override the standard configuration parameters. In this case, we set the content type and fault alerting and recovery techniques.

❑ Configuring Connections to Remote Systems

When you choose systems from the `Printer Services` menu, as shown in Figure 4-7, you will see the menu in Figure 4-8, which controls remote printer configurations.

Figure 4-7: LP Printer Services Menu. Choose `systems` to add, remove, and modify connections to remote printers.

```
2   Line Printer Services Configuration and Operation
---------------------------------------------------------
classes     - Manage Classes of Related Printers
filters     - Manage Filters for Special Processes
forms       - Manage Pre-printed Forms
operations- Perform Daily Printer Service Operations
printers    - Configure Printers for the Printer Service
priorities- Assign Print Queue Priorities to Users
requests    - Manage Active Print Requests
status      - Display Status of Printer Service
systems     - Configure Connection to Remote Systems
preSVR4     - Printer Setup
```

Figure 4-8: Remote System Connections Menu. Choose the menu entry that addresses the task at hand.

```
3   Configure Connection to Other Systems
---------------------------------------------------------
add         - Add a New System Connection
list        - Display Available System Connections
modify      - Modify System Connection
remove      - Remove System Connection
```

Adding a New System Connection

When a dial-out modem is used, three prerequisites must be satisfied:

- ▲ the printer must be connected through a dialed modem,
- ▲ a dial-out modem must be connected to the computer,
- ▲ the Basic Network Utilities must know about this modem.

Because the `cu` program accesses a printer in the same way the LP print service does, you should set up the files as though preparing access to the printer for `cu`. The `cu` command is not used to access printers but can serve as a yardstick when setting up files: if `cu` can access a printer, the LP print service will be able to access it, too.

Selecting `add` in the `Remote System Connections` menu brings up the dialog box shown in Figure 4-9:

```
 4      Add a New System Connection
 ----------------------------------------------------------
 System name:
 Scheduler type: s5   (or bsd)

 Connection timeout: n

 Retry Period:
```

Figure 4-9: System Connection Dialog Box.
Fill in the blanks to add a connection to a remote system to the print service. You must still add, accept, and enable the remote printer.

Enter the name of the system that the printer is connected to, and the type of print scheduler that runs on the remote system. Two strings are accepted: `s5` (for System V, the default) or `bsd` (for SunOS). The `connection timeout` period is a measure of how long the network connection can be idle before the print service drops the connection. Enter either a non-negative integer in minutes or `n`, the default, which means never time out. The `retry period` specifies how long to let the network connection stay dropped. Enter either a non-negative integer in minutes or `n`, the default, which means try to reconnect when there is work for the printer.

Other Remote Connection Operations

▲ `list` displays the defining information about each of the remotely connected systems.

▲ `modify` causes the basic definition to be displayed, allowing you to edit any of the pertinent fields.

▲ `remove` allows you to disconnect from any remotely connected printer.

❑ Adding a Printer to a Class

A group of printers can be defined to constitute a single, named *class*. When users submit a file for printing by a class, the LP print service picks the first printer in the class that it finds free. This allows faster turn-around, as printers are kept as busy as possible.

Classes are used to establish a priority ordering of equivalent printers. For example, group a high-speed printer and a low-speed printer in a single class; the high-speed printer handles as many requests as possible and the low-speed printer is reserved for use when the other is busy. This keeps both printers as busy as possible.

You must add each printer to the system before adding it to a class. Recall from Figure 4-4 that you can assign class membership while adding a new printer. You can also assign a printer to a class by selecting `classes` from the main `Printer Services` menu, as shown in Figure 4-10. Doing so will invoke the `Manage Classes` menu shown in Figure 4-11.

```
2  Line Printer Services Configuration and Operation
-----------------------------------------------------------
classes    - Manage Classes of Related Printers
filters    - Manage Filters for Special Processes
forms      - Manage Pre-printed Forms
operations - Perform Daily Printer Service Operations
printers   - Configure printers for the Printer Service
priorities - Assign Print Queue Priorities to Users
requests   - Manage Active Print Requests
status     - Display Status of Printer Service
systems    - Configure Connection to Remote Systems
preSVR4    - Printer Setup
```

Figure 4-10: Managing Printer Classes.
Choose classes *to add and remove printer from classes and to list class members.*

```
3  Manage Classes of Related Printers
----------------------------------------
add     - Add a New Class
list    - List Printers in Classes
modify  - Modify the Membership of a Class
remove  - Remove Classes
```

Figure 4-11: Menu for Managing Printer Classes.
Choose the entry that suits your task.

Selecting add displays a dialog box for the new class name and the list of printers in the class. Class names and printer names must be unique.

Selecting list displays a dialog box to enter the names of one or more print classes. The system displays the printers that comprise each class.

To modify class membership using the menu, select modify from the Classes menu. Enter the name of the class, whether you want to add or remove printers from that class (add is the default), and the names of the printers to be added or removed.

Selecting remove displays a dialog box where you can enter the names of the classes you want to remove. You can only remove a class if it has no pending print requests.

❑ Displaying Printer Configuration Information

To display configuration information about a printer, choose `list` from the `Configure Printers` menu, shown in Figure 4-2. You will be asked to provide a printer name and to choose between the long and short forms of the status information, and will see one of the following lines of output:

`printer` *printer-name* `now printing` *request.* `enabled since` *date.*

`printer` *printer-name* `is idle. enabled since` *date.*

`printer` *printer-name* `disabled since` *date.*
    reason

`printer` *printer-name* `waiting for auto-retry.`
    reason

The `waiting for auto-retry` output shows that the LP print service failed in trying to use the printer, because of the *reason* shown, and that it will try again later.

With the long form of the command, you should also see the following output:

`Form Mounted:`	*form-name*
`Content types:`	*content-type-list*
`Printer type:`	*printer-type*
`Description:`	*comment*
`Connection:`	*connection-info*
`Interface:`	*pathname*
`On fault:`	*alert-method*
`After fault:`	*fault-recovery*
`Users allowed:`	*user-list*
`Forms allowed:`	*form-list*
`Banner [not] required`	
`Character set:`	*character-set-list*
`Default pitch:`	*integer* `CPI,` *integer* `LPI`
`Default page size:`	*scaled-decimal-number* `wide,`
	scaled-decimal-number `long`
`Default port settings:`	*stty-option-list*

❏ Modifying a Printer Configuration

You may modify a printer's configuration by selecting `modify` from the `Configure Printers` menu shown in Figure 4-3. Doing so invokes the `Modify Printer` menu shown in Figure 4-12. The `configure` and `comm-setup` options bring up the dialog boxes shown in Figures 4-4 and 4-5, respectively.

```
4  Modify Printer printer-id
----------------------------------------
access     - Printer Access Setup
comm-setup- Local Printer Communication Parameters
configure  - Local Printer Configuration Parameters
configure  - Remote Printer Configuration Parameters
charset    - Software Selectable Character Set Aliases
printwheel- Removable Print Wheel Name
```

Figure 4-12: Mo dify Printer Configuration Menu. Choose the menu entry that addresses the task at hand.

❏ Removing a Printer

To remove a printer using the menus, select `remove` from the `Configure Printer` menu, shown in Figure 4-3. This will display a dialog box that prompts you for the names of the printers to be deleted. If you say all, only those printers with no queued requests will be removed. Removing the last printer in a class automatically removes the class as well.

❏ Printer Setup (Backwards Compatibility)

Selecting `preSVR4` from the `Printer Services` menu allows you to include a specific set of backwards compatible applications.

When you make that selection, you are presented with the warning shown in

Figure 4-13. Should you continue, the `preSVR4` menu selections for filters, forms and printwheels are made available to you.

Figure 4-13: Ba ckwards Com- patibility Warning.
You may need to continue using pre-SVR4 add-on packages that depend on an out- dated interface with the LP Print Service. If so,

```
3     Warning
------------------------------------------------
Please note that the following menus are intended
to provide backwards compatibility for preSVR4 add-on
packages that depend on the existence of the preSVR4
FACE user interface.

It is recommended that you use the other selections
provided in the Line Printer Configuration and Operation
menu if your package is release 4.0 compatible.
```

5

Customizing the Print Service

❑ Overview

Although the LP print service tries to be flexible enough to handle most print-ers and printing needs, you may buy a printer that doesn't quite fit into the way the print service handles printers or you may have a printing need that the standard features of the print service won't accommodate.

You can customize the print service in several ways. This chapter tells you how you can

▲ adjust the printer port characteristics

▲ adjust the `terminfo` database

▲ write an interface program

Another way to customize the LP print service is to write or modify a filter. See Chapter 9, *Filters*, for more information.

The diagram in Figure 5-1 gives an overview of print request processing.

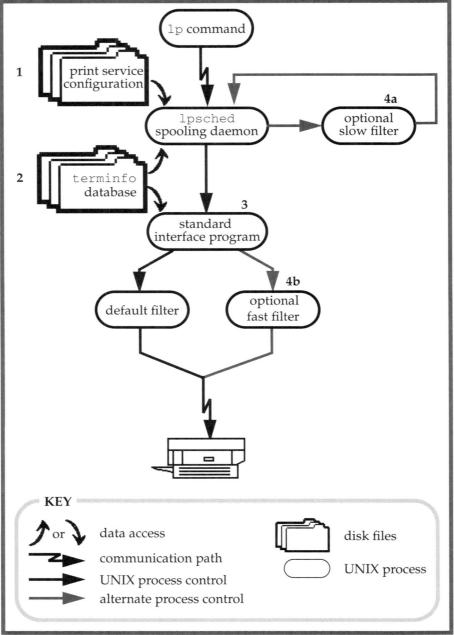

Figure 5-1: How LP Processes the Print Request
`lp -d laser file`

Each print request is sent to a spooling daemon that keeps track of all the requests. The daemon is created when you start the LP print service. This UNIX system process is also responsible for keeping track of the status of the printers and slow filters; when a printer finishes printing a user's file, the daemon will start it printing another request, if one is queued.

You can customize the print service by adjusting or replacing some of the pieces shown in Figure 5-1. (The numbers in the following list are keyed to the diagram.)

1. For most printers, you need only change the printer configuration stored on disk. Earlier chapters, *Configuring Printers* and *Using Menus to Configure Printers*, have explained how to do this. Some of the more printer-dependent configuration data are the printer port characteristics: baud rate, parity, and so on.

2. For printers that are not represented in the `terminfo` database, you can add a new entry that describes the capabilities of the printer. This database is used in two parallel capacities: screening print requests to ensure that those accepted can be handled by the desired printer and setting the printer in a state where it is ready to print the request.

   For instance, if the `terminfo` database does not show a printer capable of setting a page length requested by a user, the spooling daemon will reject the request. On the other hand, if it does show it capable, then the same information will be used by the interface program to initialize the printer.

3. For particularly difficult printers or if you want to add features not provided by the delivered LP print service, you can change the standard interface program. This program is responsible for managing the printer: it prints the banner page, initializes the printer, and invokes a filter to send copies of the user's files to the printer.

4. (both 4a. and 4b.) To provide a link between the applications used on your system and the printers, you can add slow and fast filters. Each type of filter can convert a file into another form, mapping one set of escape sequences into another, for instance, and can provide special setup by interpreting print modes requested by a user. Slow filters are run separately by the daemon to avoid tying up a printer. Fast filters are run so their output goes directly to the printer; thus, they can exert control over the printer.

❑ Adjusting the Printer Port Characteristics

You should make sure that the printer port characteristics set by the LP print service match the printer communication settings. The standard printer port settings have been designed to work with typical files and many printers, but they won't work with all files and printers. This isn't really a customizing step, because a standard feature of the LP print service is to allow you to specify the port settings for each printer. However, it's an important step in getting your printer to work with the LP print service, so it's described in more detail here.

When you add a new printer, read the documentation that comes with it so that you understand what it expects from the host (the LP print service). Then read the manual page for the stty(1) command in the *UNIX System V Release 4 System Administrator's Guide*. It summarizes the various characteristics that can be set on a terminal or printer port.

Only some of the characteristics listed in the stty(1) manual page are important for printers. The ones likely to be of interest to you are listed below (but you should still consult the stty(1) manual page for others).

Figure 5-2: stty Options that Apply to Printers. These are the stty options most likely to be used to characterize a printer.

stty Option	Meaning
evenp	Send even parity in the 8th bit
oddp	Send odd parity in the 8th bit
-parity	Don't generate parity; send all 8 bits unchanged
110 to 38400	Set the communications speed to this baud rate
ixon	Enable XON/XOFF (also known as START/STOP or DC1/DC3) flow control
-ixon	Turn off XON/XOFF flow control
-opost	Don't do any output post-processing
opost	Do output post-processing according to the settings listed below
onlcr	Send a carriage return before every linefeed
-onlcr	Don't send a carriage return before every linefeed
ocrnl	Change carriage returns into linefeeds
-ocrnl	Don't change carriage returns into linefeeds
-tabs	Change tabs into an equivalent number of spaces
tabs	Don't change tabs into spaces

When you have a set of printer port characteristics you think should apply, adjust the printer configuration as described in Chapter 3, *Configuring Printers*. You may find that the default settings are sufficient for your printer.

❑ Adjusting the `terminfo` Database

The LP print service relies on a standard interface and the `terminfo` database to initialize each printer and establish a selected page size, character pitch, line pitch, and character set. Thus, it is usually sufficient to have the correct entry in the `terminfo` database to add a new printer to the LP print service. Several entries for AT&T printers and other popular printers are delivered in the standard `terminfo` database.

Each printer is identified in the `terminfo` database with a short name; this kind of name is identical to the kind of name used to set the `TERM` shell variable. For instance, the AT&T model 455 printer is identified by the name `455`.

The `tput` command provides a quick way to verify that the shortname you select is supported by your system. Type:

```
tput -T terminal-name longname
```

If your system supports your printer, it will respond with the complete name. Otherwise, you get an error message.

To find an acceptable name for the printer, look at `/usr/share/lib/terminfo`. The `terminfo` directory contains a collection of files with single character names. Each file, in turn, holds a list of terminal names that begin with that character. Find the file whose name matches the initial character in your printer's name, list the contents, and look for your printer.

If you cannot find a `terminfo` entry for your printer, you should add one. If you don't, you may still be able to use the printer with the LP print service but you won't have the option of automatic selection of page size, pitch, and character sets, and you may have trouble keeping the printer set in the correct modes for each print request. Another option to follow, instead of updating the `terminfo` entry, is to customize the interface program used with the printer. (See the next section for details on how to do this.)

There are hundreds of items that can be defined for each terminal or printer in the `terminfo` database. However, the LP print service uses fewer than 50 of these. The following table lists the items that need to be defined (as appropriate for the printer) to add a new printer to the LP print service.

Figure 5-3: `ter-minfo` Entries
These are the terminfo parameters that are most likely to be of interest when configuring a printer.

`terminfo` item	Meaning
Booleans:	
cpix	Changing character pitch changes resolution
daisy	Printer needs operator to change character set
lpix	Changing line pitch changes resolution
Numbers:	
bufsz	Number of bytes buffered before printing
cols	Number of columns in a line
cps	Average print rate in characters per second
it	Tabs initially every # spaces
lines	Number of lines on a page
orc	Horizontal resolution in units per character
orhi	Horizontal resolution in units per inch
orl	Vertical resolution in units per line
orvi	Vertical resolution in units per inch
Strings:	
chr	Change horizontal resolution
cpi	Change number of characters per inch
cr	Carriage return
csnm	List of character set names
cud1	Down one line
cud	Move carriage down # lines
cuf	Move carriage right # columns
cuf1	Carriage right
cvr	Change vertical resolution
ff	Page eject
hpa	Horizontal position absolute
ht	Tab to next 8-space tab stop
if	Name of initialization file
iprog	Path name of initializing program
is1	Printer initialization string
is2	Printer initialization string
is3	Printer initialization string
lpi	Change number of lines per inch

`terminfo` item	Meaning
mgc	Clear all margins (top, bottom, and sides)
rep	Repeat a character # times
rwidm	Disable double wide printing
scs	Select character set
scsd	Start definition of a character set
slines	Set page length to # lines per page
smgl	Set left margin at current column
smglp	Set left margin
smgr	Set right margin at current column
smgrp	Set right margin
smglr	Set both left and right margins
smgt	Set top margin at current line
smgtp	Set top margin
smgb	Set bottom margin at current line
smgbp	Set bottom margin
smgtb	Set both top and bottom margins
swidm	Enable double wide printing
vpa	Vertical position absolute

To construct a database entry for a new printer, see details about the structure of the `terminfo` database in the `terminfo`(4) manual page (*UNIX System V System Files and Devices Reference Manual*).

Once you've made the new entry, you need to compile it into the database using the `tic`(1) command. Just enter the following command:

    `tic` *file-name*

where *file-name* is the name of the file containing the `terminfo` entry you have crafted for the new printer.

◆ *Note*   The LP print service gains much efficiency by caching information from the `terminfo` database. If you add or delete `terminfo` entries, or change the values that govern pitch settings, page size, or character sets, you should stop and restart the print service so it can read the new information. See Chapter 6, *Administering the Print Service*.

❑ Modifying the Interface Program

◆ *Note*   If you have an interface program that you have used with the LP
                  Spooling Utilities before UNIX System V Release 3.2, it should still
                  work with the LP print service. Note, though, that several -o
                  options have been standardized, and will be passed to every inter-
                  face program. These may interfere with similarly named options
                  used by your interface.

If you have a printer that is not supported by simply adding an entry to the
`terminfo` database, or if you have printing needs that are not supported by
the standard interface program, you can furnish your own interface program.
It is a good idea to start with the standard interface program, and change it to
fit, rather than starting from scratch. You can find a copy of it under the name

```
/usr/lib/lp/model/standard
```

What Does the Interface Program Do?

Any interface program is responsible for doing the following tasks:

▲   Initializing the printer port, if necessary. The generic interface pro-
    gram uses the `stty` command to do this.

▲   Initializing the physical printer. The generic interface program uses
    the `terminfo` database and the `TERM` shell variable to get the control
    sequences to do this.

▲   Printing a banner page, if necessary.

▲   Printing the correct number of copies of the request content.

An interface program is not responsible for opening the printer port. The LP
print service opens the port, including calling a dial-up printer i f necessary.
The printer port connection is given to the interface program as standard output, and the printer is identified as the controlling terminal for the interface
program. A "hang-up" on the port will cause a `SIGHUP` signal to be sent to
the interface program.

A customized interface program must not terminate the connection to the printer and must leave it in its initial state.

How Is the Interface Program Used?

When the LP print service routes an output request to a printer, the interface program for the printer is invoked as follows:

```
/etc/lp/interfaces/printer request-id user title copies \
    options file1 file2 ...
```

where *printer* is a printer name, *request-id* is the request ID returned by the `lp`(1) command, *user* is the login name of the user who made the request, *title* is an optional title specified by the user, *copies* is the number of copies requested by the user, *options* is a blank-separated list of options specified by the user or set by the LP print service, and *file1, file2, ...* are full pathnames of the files to be printed.

When the interface program is invoked, its standard input comes from `/dev/null`, its standard output is directed to the printer port, and its standard error output is directed to a file that will be given to the user who submitted the print request.

The standard interface recognizes the following values in the list in *options:*

Option	Meaning and Use
Figure 5-4: Inter face Program Options. These are options that are recognized by the standard interface program.	
nobanner	Suppress the printing of a banner page. The default is to print one.
nofilebreak	Skip page breaks between separate data files. By default, a page break is made between each file in the print request.
cpi=*decimal-number$_1$* lpi=*decimal-number$_2$*	Print with *decimal-number$_1$* columns per inch and *decimal-number$_2$* lines per inch, respectively. The standard interface program extracts the control sequences needed to initialize the printer to handle the character and line pitches from the terminfo database.

The words pica, elite, and compressed are acceptable replacements for *decimal-number$_1$* and are synonyms for 10 columns per inch, 12 columns per inch, and as many columns per inch as possible. |
| length=*decimal-number$_1$* width=*decimal-number$_2$* | These options specify the length and width, respectively, of the pages to be printed. The standard interface program extracts the control sequences needed to initialize the printer to handle the page length and page width from the terminfo database. |
| stty='*stty-option-list*' | The *stty-option-list* is applied after a default *stty-option-list* as arguments to the command. The default list is used to establish a default port configuration; the additional list given to the interface program is used to change the configuration as needed. |

The above options are either specified by the user when issuing a print request or by the LP print service from defaults given by the administrator for the printer (cpi, lpi, length, width, stty) or for the pre-printed form used in the request (cpi, lpi, length, width).

Additional printer configuration information is passed to the interface pro-gram in shell variables:

Shell Variable	Meaning and Use
TERM=*printer-type*	Specifies the type of printer. The value is used as a key for getting printer capability information from the extended terminfo database.
FILTER='*pipeline*'	Specifies the filter to use to send the request content to the printer; the filter is given control of the printer.
CHARSET=*character-set*	Specifies the character set to be used when printing the content of a print request. The standard interface pro-gram extracts the control sequences needed to select the character set from the terminfo database.

Figure 5-5: Shell Variables Speci-fying Configura-tion Information. These are shell variables that con-tain printer service parameters.

A customized interface program should either ignore these options and shell variables or should recognize them and treat them in a consistent manner.

Customizing the Interface Program

Make sure that the custom interface program sets the proper stty modes (terminal characteristics such as baud rate and output options). The standard interface program does this, and you can follow suit. Look for the section that begins with the shell comment

```
## Initialize the printer port
```

Follow the code used in the standard interface program. It sets both the default modes and the adjusted modes given by either the LP print service or the user with a line such as the following:

```
stty mode options 0<&1
```

This command line takes the standard input for the stty command from the printer port. An example of a stty command line that sets the baud rate at 1200 and sets some of the option modes is shown below:

```
stty -parenb -parodd 1200 cs8 cread clocal ixon 0<&1
```

One printer port characteristic not set by the standard interface program is hardware flow control. The way that this is set will vary, depending on your computer hardware. The code for the standard interface program suggests where hardware flow control and other printer port characteristics can be set. Look for the section that begins with the shell comment

```
# Here you may want to add other port initialization
code.
```

Because different printers have different numbers of columns, make sure the header and trailer for your interface program correspond to your printer. The standard interface program prints a banner that fits on an 80-column page (except for the user's title, which may be longer). Look in the code for the standard interface program for the section that begins with the shell comment

```
## Print the banner page
```

Some applications, when run with certain printers, may require that you turn off page breaking. If you must turn off page breaking, you can modify the standard interface program (/usr/lib/lp/model/standard) at line 921 by changing the "no" to "yes."

The custom interface program should print all user related error messages on the standard output or on the standard error. The messages sent to the standard error will be mailed to the user; the messages printed on the standard output will end up on the printed page where they can be read by the user when he or she picks up the output.

When printing is complete, your interface program should exit with a code that shows the status of the print job. Exit codes are interpreted by the LP print service as follows:

Code	Meaning to the LP print service
0	The print request has been completed successfully. If a printer fault has occurred, it has been cleared.
1 to 127	A problem has been encountered in printing this particular request (for example, too many non-printable characters, or the request exceeds the printer capabilities). The LP print service notifies the person who submitted the request that there was an error in printing it. This problem will not affect future print requests. If a printer fault had occurred, it has been cleared.
128	Reserved for internal use by the LP print service. Interface programs must not exit with this code.
129	A printer fault has been encountered in printing the request. This problem will affect future print requests. If the fault recovery for the printer directs the LP print service to wait for the administrator to fix the problem, the LP print service will disable the printer. If the fault recovery is to continue printing, the LP print service will not disable the printer, but will try printing again in a few minutes.
> 129	These codes are reserved for internal use by the LP print service. Interface programs must not exit with codes in this range.

Figure 5-6: Exit Codes
The interface program will exit with a code that shows the status of the print job.

As Figure 5-6 shows, one way of alerting the administrator to a printer fault is to exit with a code of 129. Unfortunately, if the interface program exits, the LP print service has no choice but to reprint the request from the beginning when the fault has been cleared. Another way of getting an alert to the administrator (that does not require the entire request to be reprinted) is to have the interface program send a fault message to the LP print service but wait for the fault to clear. When the fault clears, the interface program can resume printing the user's file. When the printing is finished, the interface program can give a zero exit code just as if the fault had never occurred. An added advantage is that the interface program can detect when the fault is cleared automatically, so that the administrator doesn't have to enable the printer.

Fault messages can be sent to the LP print service using the `lp.tell` program. This is referenced using the `$LPTELL` shell variable in the standard interface code. The program takes its standard input and sends it to the LP print service where it is put into the message that alerts the administrator to the printer fault. If its standard input is empty, `lp.tell` does not initiate an alert. Examine the standard interface code immediately after these comments for an example of how the `lp.tell` (`$LPTELL`) program is used:

```
# Here's where we set up the $LPTELL program to capture
# fault messages.


# Here's where we print the file.
```

If the special exit code 129 or the `lp.tell` program is used, there is no longer a need for the interface program to disable the printer itself. Your interface program can disable the printer directly, but doing so will override the fault alerting mechanism. Alerts are sent only if the LP print service detects the printer has faulted, and the special exit code and the `lp.tell` program are its main detection tools.

If the LP print service has to interrupt the printing of a file at any time, it will kill the interface program with a signal `TERM` (trap number 15; see `kill`(1) and `signal`(2) in the *UNIX System V Release 4 User's Reference Manual/System Administrator's Reference Manual* and *UNIX System V Programmer's Reference Manual: Operating System API*, respectively). If the interface program dies from receipt of any other signal, the LP print service assumes that future print requests won't be affected and continues to use the printer. The LP print service notifies the person who submitted the request that the request has not been finished successfully.

When the interface is first invoked, the signals `HUP`, `INT`, `QUIT`, and `PIPE` (trap numbers 1, 2, 3, and 13) are ignored. The standard interface changes this so that these signals are trapped at appropriate times. The standard interface interprets receipt of these signals as warnings that the printer has a problem; when it receives one, it issues a fault alert.

6

Administering the Printer Service

❏ Overview

Once you have installed your print service, defined and properly configured all the printers, and customized the print service to suit your system configuration and user requirements, you can sit back and watch the print service manage printers and print requests smoothly, efficiently, effortlessly …until something goes wrong. This chapter presents the housekeeping tasks that are generally performed throughout the day. The next chapter deals with techniques for managing the queue of print requests. These two groups of tasks make the LP administrator's job an ongoing one.

So what are these housekeeping tasks you can look forward to? Suppose a printer is scheduled for a checkup by the field service rep this morning, and the guy actually shows up. You will need to disable the printer until the printer is operational again. Suppose the printer is the system default destination. You might want to set a new one for the time being. And then there are the forms, print wheels, and character sets that pesky users want you to mount…

These are the operations that are generally performed throughout the day as necessary:

▲   accepting and rejecting requests to certain printers

▲   disabling and re-enabling certain printers

▲   starting and stopping the printer service

▲   mounting and unmounting forms, print wheels, and character sets

▲   setting the default print destination

▲   examining the status of the print service

The shell commands used to do daily administrative tasks are `accept` and `reject`, `enable` and `disable`, and `lpsched`, `lpshut`, and `lpmove`. The menu interface is through the `operations` entry in the `Printer Services` menu, as shown in Figure 6-1 and Figure 6-2. Both the shell commands and the menus are presented.

Figure 6-1: Daily Print Service Maintenance. Choose `opera-tions` *to perform print service main-tenance activities like enabling and disabling printers, accepting and rejecting print requests, and start-ing and stopping the print service.*

```
2  Line Printer Services Configuration and Operation
----------------------------------------------------------
classes        - Manage Classes of Related Printers
filters        - Manage Filters for Special Processes
forms          - Manage Pre-printed Forms
operations     - Perform Daily Printer Service Operations
printers       - Configure Printers for the Printer Service
priorities     - Assign Print Queue Priorities to Users
requests       - Manage Active Print Requests
status         - Display Status of Printer Service
systems        - Configure Connection to Remote Systems
preSVR4        - Printer Setup
```

```
3        Perform Daily Printer Service Operations
----------------------------------------------------------------
-
accept     - Allow Class(es) and/or Printer(s) to Accept Print
Requests
control    - Start (Stop) the Printer Service
disable    - Disable Printer from Printing
enable     - Enable Printer for Printing
mount      - Mount Form or Font on a Printer
reject     - Stop a Printer from Accepting Print Requests
set default- Set the Default Printer Destination
unmount    - Unmount a Form or a print wheel from a Printer
```

Figure 6-2:Daily Print Service Administration Menu.
Select the menu entry suited to the maintenance task at hand.

❑ Accepting and Rejecting Print Requests for a Printer or Class

When a new printer or class is added to the print service, or after a printer has been classified as not accepting requests, you must tell the LP Print Service to start accepting requests for the printer or class.

After the condition that led to denying requests has been corrected or changed, or when the new printer or class has been added and configured, either select accept from the Daily Administration menu (see Figure 6-2) and name the printer or class to be restarted, or enter the following command:

    accept *printer-or-class-name*

You can accept requests for several printers or classes in one command by listing their names on the same line.

To stop accepting any new requests for a printer or class of printers, enter the following command to the shell:

```
reject -r "reason" printer-or-class-name
```

To reject requests for several printers or classes in one command, list their names on the same line, separating the names with spaces. The *reason* will be displayed whenever anyone tries to print a file on the printer. If you don't want to give a reason, don't use -r.

If you use menu selection, select reject from the Daily Administration menu (see Figure 6-2). Then enter the names of the printers and classes for which to reject requests in the dialog box that appears. You may also enter a *reason* for rejecting requests.

Any requests currently queued for the printer will continue to print as long as the printer is enabled.

❑ Enabling and Disabling a Printer

When a new printer is added to the print service, or after a printer has been disabled, you must enable the printer to resume printing.

After the condition that led to the printer being disabled has been corrected, or when the new printer has been added and configured, either select enable from the Daily Administration menu (see Figure 6-2) and name the printer to be restarted, or enter the following command:

```
enable printer-name
```

◆ *Note*   At installation you may allow all users to enable and disable printers. See *Installing the LP Print Service* in Chapter 2.

Selecting disable in the Daily Administration menu (see Figure 6-2) will cause the specified printer to stop printing immediately. When you select this option, you will fill in the following dialog box:

```
4   Disable Printer from Printing
-----------------------------------------------
Printer:
What should happen to any requests pending?   restart
Reason for disabling:
```

*Figure 6-3: Dis-
able Printer
Dialog Box.*
*Fill in the printer
name, the reason
the printer is dis-
abled, and a dispo-
sition for pending
print requests.*

The command to disable a printer is:

disable [-c] [-W] [-r [*reason*]] *printers*

By default, any requests that are currently printing on the designated *printers* will be reprinted in their entirety on either the same printer or another printer in the same class. If a printer is a remote one, typing disable will halt the transmission of jobs to the remote system. The disable command must be run on the remote system to halt the remote printer.

Use -c or enter cancel (if you're using the menu interface) to cancel any requests that are currently printing on the designated *printers*. Use -W to wait until the request currently being printed is finished before disabling the printer. These two options are mutually exclusive: you cannot specify them both. If the printer is remote, -c and -W have no effect.

You can also specify a reason for the printer being disabled; it will be displayed whenever anyone tries to print a file on the printer. If you don't want to give a reason, don't use -r.

❑ Starting and Stopping the Printer Service

Under normal operation, you should never have to start or stop the LP print service manually. It is automatically started each time the UNIX system is booted, and stopped each time the UNIX system is brought down. If, however, you need to stop the LP print service without stopping the UNIX system, follow the procedure described below.

Stopping the LP print service will cause all printing to cease within seconds. Any print requests that have not finished printing will be printed in their entirety after the LP print service is restarted. The printer configurations, forms, and filters in effect when the LP print service is stopped will be restored after it is restarted.

◆ *Note*   To start and stop the LP print service manually, you must be logged in as either the user lp or the superuser root.

Manually Stopping the Print Service

To stop the LP print service manually, enter the following command:

```
lpshut
```

The message

```
Print services stopped.
```

will appear, and all printing will cease within a few seconds. If you try to stop the LP print service when it is not running, you will see the message

```
Print services already stopped.
```

Manually Starting the Print Service

To restart the LP print service manually, enter the following command:

```
lpsched
```

The message

```
Print services started.
```

will appear. There may be some delay while the printer configurations, forms, and filters are reestablished before any saved print requests start printing. If you try to restart the LP print service when it is already running, you will see the message

```
Print services already active.
```

◆ *Note*   The LP print service does not have to be stopped to change printer configurations or to add forms or filters.

❏ Mounting and Unmounting Forms, Print Wheels, or Character Sets

◆ *Note*   See Chapter 8, *Pre-printed Forms*, for more information about pre-printed forms, and Chapter 3, *Configuring Printers*, for more about print wheels and character sets.

Before the LP print service can start printing files that need a pre-printed form, print wheel, or character set, you must physically mount the form, print wheel, or character set on a printer, and notify the LP print service that you have mounted it. If alerting has been set on the form or print wheel, you will be alerted when enough print requests are queued waiting for it to be mounted. (See *Alerting to Mount a Print Wheel* in Chapter 3 and *Alerting to Mount a Form* in Chapter 8.)

The proper mount procedure has these three steps:

1. **Disable the printer**, using the `disable` command. If you don't, the print service will continue to use the printer. It is difficult to mount a form on a printer that's currently printing

2. **Mount the new form, print wheel, or character set**. Physically load the new form, print wheel, or character set into the printer. Then enter the following command to tell the LP print service it has been mounted. (The following command line is split into two lines for readability.)

```
lpadmin -p printer-name -M [ -S print-wheel-name ] \
    [ -f form-name [ -a [ -o filebreak ]]]
```

Leave out the -S *print-wheel-name* if you are mounting only a form, or leave out the -f *formname* -a -o filebreak if you are mounting only a print wheel.

If you are mounting a form with an alignment pattern defined for it, you will be asked to press the (return) key before each copy of the alignment pattern is printed. After the pattern is printed, you can adjust the printer and press the (return) key again. If no alignment pattern has been defined, you won't be asked to press the (return) key. You can drop the -a -o filebreak if you don't want to bother with the alignment pattern.

The -o filebreak option tells the LP print service to add a form-feed after each copy of the alignment pattern. The actual control sequence used for the formfeed depends on the printer involved and is obtained from the terminfo database. If the alignment pattern already includes a formfeed, leave out the -o filebreak option.

3. **Re-enable the printer**, using the enable command.

If you want to unmount a form or print wheel, use the following command:

```
lpadmin -p printer-name -M -S none -f none
```

Leave out the option -S none if you just want to unmount a form. Similarly, leave out the -f none option if you just want to unmount a print wheel.

Until you've mounted a form on a printer, only print requests that don't require a form will be printed. Likewise, until you've mounted a print wheel on a printer, only print requests that don't require a particular print wheel will be printed. Print requests that do require a particular form or print wheel will be held in a queue until the form or print wheel is mounted.

You can use the Daily Administration menu (Figure 6-2) to mount and unmount forms and print wheels as well. Choosing mount causes the dialog box in Figure 6-4 to be displayed (Note: a *font* and a *print wheel* are synonymous):

```
4    Mount Form or Font
----------------------------------
Printer:
Form to be mounted:
Print wheel to be mounted:
Print an alignment pattern: no
```

Figure 6-4: Mount Form or Font Dialog Box. Fill in the printer name, form name, and whether to print an alignment pattern. You can mount both a form and a print wheel on a printer in one operation.

Selecting unmount from the Daily Administration menu (Figure 6-2) allows you to specify that a form or font on a specified printer is to be unmounted.

❏ Setting the Default Destination

Selecting set default from the Daily Administration menu (Figure 6-2) allows you to specify the destination of print requests when it is not specifically given. The printer or class must already exist.

You may also do this by setting the LPDEST shell variable, or with a shell command:

```
lpadmin -d printer-or-class-name
```

If you later decide that there should be no default destination, enter a null *printer-or-class-name* as in the following command:

```
lpadmin -d
```

If you don't set a default destination, there will be none. Users will either have to name a specific printer or class in each print request (using lp -d), or set their LPDEST shell variable with the name of a default destination printer.

❏ Displaying the Status of Printer Service

Selecting the `Display Status` option from the `Printer Services` menu brings up the menu shown in Figure 6-5.

Figure 6-5: Print Service Status Menu.
You can display the available forms, printers, print wheels and character sets, and a list of the pending requests.

```
3   Display Status of Printer Services
-------------------------------------------------
forms       - Display Forms Status
printers    - Display Printers Status
requests    - Status of Print Requests
wheels      - Status of Print wheels and Character Sets
```

Select `forms` for a list of the forms that are currently available to you. Select `printers` to see the status of each printer. Select `requests` to examine a list of currently pending print requests. Select `wheels` to see a list of the available character sets and print wheels.

Alternatively, use the following shell command to list your printers:

```
lpstat -t
```

❏ More about `lpsched`, `lpshut`, and `lpmove`

The commands `lpsched`, `lpshut`, and `lpmove` have been shown in preceding sections as solutions to specific tasks the LP administrator encounters. This section presents the complete set of options of each of these commands, and can be used as a reference.

`lpsched` starts the LP print service; this can be done only by users `root` or `lp`. The command has no arguments:

```
lpsched
```

`lpshut` shuts down the print service. All printers that are printing at the time `lpshut` is invoked will stop printing. When `lpsched` is started again, requests that were printing at the time a printer was shut down will be reprinted from the beginning. To stop the LP print service, type

```
lpshut
```

`lpmove` moves requests that were queued by `lp` between printer destinations. Two forms of the command can be used:

```
lpmove requests dest
lpmove dest1 dest2
```

The first form of the `lpmove` command shown above moves the *requests* to the printer *dest*. The *requests* are request-IDs as returned by `lp`. The second form of the command will attempt to move all requests for destination *dest$_1$* to destination *dest$_2$*; `lp` will then reject any new requests for *dest$_1$*.

Note that when moving requests, `lpmove` never checks the acceptance status (see the preceding section *Accepting and Rejecting Print Requests for a Printer or Class*) of the new destination. Also, the request-IDs of the moved request are not changed, so that users can still find their requests. The `lpmove` command will not move requests that have options (content type, form required, and so on) that cannot be handled by the new destination.

If a request was originally queued for a class or the special destination `any`, and the first form of `lpmove` was used, the destination of the request will be changed to *new-destination*. A request thus affected will be printable only on *new-destination* and not on other members of the same class or other acceptable printers.

7

Managing the
Print Load

❏ Overview

Occasionally you may need to stop accepting print requests for a printer or move print requests from one printer to another. There are various reasons why you might want to do this, such as the need for periodic maintenance, a broken printer, a removed printer, a changed configuration or an imbalance in request loads. If the printer will be out of service for only a short time, use the procedures in the preceding chapter, *Administering the Print Service*, for enabling and disabling printers, accepting and rejecting print requests, and starting and stopping the print service.

If you are going to make a big change in the way the printer is to be used, such as stopping its ability to handle a certain form, changing the print wheels available for it, or disallowing some users from using it, print requests that are currently queued for printing on it will have to be moved or canceled. The LP print service will attempt to find alternate printers, but only if the user doesn't care which printer is to be used. Requests for a specific printer won't be automatically moved; if you don't move them first, the print service will cancel them.

This chapter describes administrative tasks connected with the request queues:

▲ cancelling requests

▲ holding and releasing requests

▲ moving requests to a different printer

▲ assigning priorities to requests

▲ changing the priority of a request

▲ moving a request to the head of the queue

▲ cleaning out the request log

You may manage the request queues by command or by selecting `requests` from the `Printer Services` menu, shown in Figure 7-1. The `Active Print Requests` menu is shown in Figure 7-2.

Figure 7-1: Managing the Print Request Queues.
Choose
requests to
cancel, hold,
release, and move
print requests.

```
2   Line Printer Services Configuration and Operation
-----------------------------------------------------------
classes       - Manage Classes of Related Printers
filters       - Manage Filters for Special Processes
forms         - Manage Pre-printed Forms
operations    - Perform Daily Printer Service Operations
printers      - Configure Printers for the Printer Service
priorities    - Assign Print Queue Priorities to Users
requests      - Manage Active Print Requests
status        - Display Status of Printer Service
systems       - Configure Connection to Remote Systems
preSVR4       - Printer Setup
```

Figure 7-2: Active Print Requests Menu.
Choose the entry
best suited to the
task at hand.

```
3       Manage Active Print Requests
-----------------------------------------------------------
cancel  - Cancel Print Requests
hold    - Place Pending Print Requests on Hold
move    - Move Print Requests to a New Destination
release - Release Held Print Requests
```

❑ Canceling Print Requests

To cancel a print request, type these commands:

```
lpstat -o
```

gets the request identification (*request-id*). Then use

```
cancel  request-id
```

If a particular request keeps getting canceled incorrectly, type the following command:

```
lpshut | cd /var/spool/lp | find requests tmp ! \
    -type d ! -name .SEQF -exec rm {}; lpsched
```

You can also cancel print requests for specific printers by selecting `cancel` in the `Active Print Requests` menu shown in Figure 7-2 and then entering the names of affected printers.

❑ Putting a Request on Hold

Any request that has not finished printing can be put on hold. You can stop its printing, if it currently is printing, and keep it from printing until you resume it. A user can also put his or her own request on hold and then resume it, but cannot resume a print request you have put on hold.

Use the following command to place a request on hold:

```
lp -i  request-id  -H hold
```

❏ Releasing Held Print Requests

To release held print requests, type:

```
lp -i request-id -H resume
```

Once resumed, a request continues to move up the queue and will eventually print. If it had been printing when you held it, it will be the next request to print. Normally it will start printing from the beginning, with page one, but you can have it start printing at a later page. Enter the following command to resume the request at a different page:

```
lp -i request-id -H resume -P starting-page -
```

The final dash is needed to specify the starting page and all subsequent pages.

You can also release the held request by selecting `release` from the `Active Print Requests` menu shown in Figure 7-2.

◆ *Note*   The ability to print a subset of pages requires the presence of a filter that can handle this. The default filter used by the LP print service does not. An attempt to resume a request on a later page will be rejected if an appropriate filter is not being used.

❏ Moving Requests to A New Destination

If you have to move requests from one printer or class to another, either select `move` from the `Print Requests` menu or enter one of the following commands:

```
lpmove request-id printer-name
lpmove printer-name1 printer-name2
```

You can give more than one request ID before the printer name in the first command.

The first command above moves the listed requests to the printer named. The second command moves *all* requests currently queued for the first printer to the second printer. When the second form is used, the print service will also no longer accept requests for the first printer.

If you select `move` from the menu, you will fill in a form with the printers to be moved from, the IDs of the requests to be moved (the default is `all`), and the new printer destination identification.

❑ Assigning Print Queue Priorities to Users and Requests

The LP print service provides a simple priority mechanism that allows users to adjust the position of a print request in the queue. Each print request can be given a priority level (a number from 0 to 39, where 0 is the highest), by the person who submits it. Thus, a user could submit a large print job with a low priority to guarantee that the job won't be printed until all the higher priority (and presumably shorter) requests are printer. The LP administrator defines the following characteristics of the priority mechanism:

▲ Each user can be assigned a personal priority limit. A user cannot submit a print request with a priority higher than the limit.

▲ A default priority limit can be assigned for users not assigned a personal limit.

▲ A default priority can be set for print requests to which the user does not assign a priority.

Use the following command to assign priority levels to individual users:

```
lpusers -q priority-level -u user-name
```

Set the limit for a group of users by listing their names after the `-u` option. Separate multiple names with a comma or space. If you use a space to separate users, enclose the whole list in quotes. To modify a user's priority limit, re-enter the `lpusers` command with a new limit. To restore a user's priority limit to the default value, enter:

```
lpusers -u user-name
```

Type the following command to set a default limit:

```
lpusers -q priority-level
```

The *priority-level* is a number from 0 to 39, with the lower numbers having higher priority, and applies to those users who have not been given a specific limit. If you do not set a default priority, the print service will use the default of 20.

To set the default priority that is assigned to print requests submitted without a priority. Use the following command:

```
lpusers -d priority-level
```

This default is applied when a user doesn't have an individual priority level. If the default priority is greater than the limit for a user, the limit is used instead.

To examine all the settings you have assigned for priority limits and defaults, type the following command:

```
lpusers -l
```

Assigning Print Queue Priorities by Menu

Choose priorities from the Printer Services menu as shown in Figure 7-3, to invoke the Print Queue Priorities menu shown in Figure 7-4. Choosing default sets the priority level to the system default value, which is 20. The list entry displays the information shown in Figure 7-5.Choose remove and enter the list of users whose priority limits will be removed. Set a system priority limit with the system entry. Enter the priority limit for the system. If you select users, enter a list of users followed by the new priority limit for them.

```
2   Line Printer Services Configuration and Operation
------------------------------------------------------------
classes        - Manage Classes of Related Printers
filters        - Manage Filters for Special Processes
forms          - Manage Pre-printed Forms
operations     - Perform Daily Printer Service Operations
printers       - Configure Printers for the Printer Service
priorities     - Assign Print Queue Priorities to Users
requests       - Manage Active Print Requests
status         - Display Status of Printer Service
systems        - Configure Connection to Remote Systems
preSVR4        - Printer Setup
```

Figure 7-3: Managing Print Queue Priorities.
Choose `priorities` to set default print request priorities and assign priority limits to individual users.

```
3   Assign Print Queue Priorities to Users
------------------------------------------------------------
default    - Set System Default Priority
list       - List Priority Limits for Users
remove     - Remove Users Priority Limit
system     - Set System Priority Limit
users      - Set User(s) Priority Limit
```

Figure 7-4: Print Queue Priorities Menu.
Choose the entry best suited to the task at hand.

```
4   Priority Limits for Users
--------------------------------
Default priority is <default-priority>
Priority limit for users not listed below is 0

          Priority        Users
             p1            u1, u2, ...
             p2            u3
              .             .
              .             .
              .             .
```

Figure 7-5: Output from List Priority Limits Menu Selection.
When you choose `list` from the `Print Queue Priorities` menu, this is what you see.

❏ Changing the Priority for a Request

Print requests that are still waiting to print can be reassigned a new priority. This overrides any existing priorities and will reposition the request in the queue to put it ahead of lower priority requests or behind any others at the same or higher priority.

Enter the following to change the priority of a request:

    lp -i *request-id* -q *new-priority-level*

You can change only one request at a time with this command. If a request is already printing, you cannot change its priority.

❏ Moving a Request to the Head of the Queue

Occasionally, you may need to move a print request to the head of the queue, making it the next one eligible for printing. If it must start printing immediately but another request is currently printing, you can hold the other request as described above.

Enter the following command to move a print request to the head of the queue:

    lp -i *request-id* -H immediate

Only privileged users lp and root can move a print request to the head of the queue; ordinary users cannot use the -H immediate option.

If you set more than one request for immediate printing, they will print in the reverse order set; that is, the request moved to the head of the queue most recently will print first.

There is no specific menu option to move a request to the head of the queue. You can achieve the same effect by following this procedure:

1. Put all requests on hold except the one you want moved. This automatically moves it to the head of the queue, since there are no other eligible entries.

2. Remove the other requests from hold.

❑ Cleaning Out the Request Log

The print service maintains files that describe each print request that is submitted for printing in the directories /var/spool/lp/tmp/*system* and /var/spool/lp/requests/*system*. The information is split into two files, one in each directory, with the more sensitive information in the /var/spool/lp/requests/*system* directory where it can be kept secure: the request file in the /var/spool/lp/tmp/*system* is safe from all except the user who submitted the request, while the file in /var/spool/lp/requests/*system* is safe from all users, including the submitting user.

These files remain in their directories only as long as the request is in the queue. Once the request is finished, the information in the files is combined and appended to the file /var/lp/logs/requests. This file is not removed by the LP print service, but can be cleaned out periodically, using, for instance, the cron facility. (See the description of the crontab command in the *UNIX System V Release 4 System Administrator's Reference Manual*.)

The default crontab entry provided with the LP print service is shown below.

```
13 3 * * * cd /var/lp/logs; if [ -f requests ]; then
   /usr/bin/mv requests xyzzy;
   /usr/bin/cp xyzzy requests; >xyzzy;
   /usr/lbin/agefile -c2 requests;
   /usr/bin/mv xyzzy requests; fi
```

(This is one line in the `crontab` but is split into several lines here for read-ability.) What this entry does, briefly, is "age" the file by changing the name to `requests-1` and moving the previous day's copy to `requests-2`. The number 2 in the `-c` option to the `agefile` program keeps the log files from the previous two days, discarding older log files. By changing this number you can change the amount of information saved. On the other hand, if you want the information to be saved more often, or if you want the file to be cleaned out more often than once a day, you can change the time when the `crontab` entry is run by changing the first two numbers. The current values, 13 and 3, cause cleaning up to be done at 3:13 A.M. each day.

The default `crontab` entry supplied is sufficient to keep the old print request records from accumulating in the spooling file system. You may want to con-dense information in the request log to produce a report on the use of the LP print service, or to aid in generating accounting information. You can produce a different script that examines the file and extracts information just before the clean up procedure.

The request log has a simple structure that makes it easy to extract data from it using common UNIX shell commands. Requests are listed in the order they are printed, and are separated by lines showing their request IDs. Each line below the separator line is marked with a single letter that identifies the kind of information contained in that line. Each letter is separated from the data by a single space. See Figure 7-6 for details.

Figure 7-6: Re-quest Log Entries.
Each entry in the request log starts with a key letter that describes the rest of the line.

Key	Contents of Line
=	This is the separator line. It contains the request ID, the user and group IDs of the user, the total number of bytes in the original (unfiltered) files, and the time when the request was queued. These items are separated by com-mas and are in the order just named. The user ID, group ID, and sizes are preceded by the words `uid`, `gid`, and `size`, respectively.
C	The number of copies printed.
D	The printer or class destination or the word `any`.
F	The name of the file printed. This line is repeated for each file that was printed and reflects the printing order.
f	The name of the form used.

Key	Contents of Line
H	One of three types of special handling: `resume`, `hold`, and `immediate`. The only useful value found in this line will be `immediate`.
N	The type of alert used when the print request was successfully completed. The type is the letter `M` if the user was notified by mail, or `W` if the user was notified by a message to his or her terminal.
O	The `-o` options.
P	The priority of the print request.
p	The list of pages printed.
r	This single letter line is included if the user asked for `raw` processing of the files (the `-r` option of the `lp` command).
S	The character set or print wheel used.
s	The outcome of the request, shown as a combination of individual bits expressed in hexadecimal form. While several bits are used internally by the print service, the most important bits are listed below: `0x0004` Slow filtering finished successfully. `0x0010` Printing finished successfully. `0x0040` The request was canceled. `0x0100` The request failed filtering or printing.
T	The title placed on the banner page.
t	The type of content found in the file(s).
U	The name of the user who submitted the print request.
x	The slow filter used for the request.
Y	The list of special modes given to the filters that printed the request.
y	The fast filter used for the request.
z	The printer used for the request. This will differ from the destination (the `D` line) if the request was queued for any printer or a class of printers, or if the request was moved to another destination by the LP print service administrator.

❑ More about `lpusers`

The `lpusers` command is used to set limits to the queue priority level that can be assigned to jobs submitted by users of the LP print service. It has been presented as a way to accomplish specific tasks in the preceding chapters. In this section, the command and all of its forms and options are presented together as a reference.

The `lpusers` command has five forms:

```
lpusers -d priority-level

lpusers -q priority-level -u user-list

lpusers -u user-list

lpusers -q priority-level

lpusers -l
```

The first form of the command (with `-d`) sets the system-wide priority default to *priority-level*, where *priority-level* is a value of 0 to 39, with 0 being the highest priority. If a user does not specify a priority level with a print request, the default priority is used. Initially, the default priority level is 20.

The second form of the command (with `-q` and `-u`) sets the default highest *priority-level* that the users in *user-list* can assign to a print request. The *user-list* argument may include any or all of the following constructs:

*Figure 7-7: User -list Arguments The **user-list** argument to* `lpusers` *may include any or all of these constructs.*

Item	Meaning
user	A specific user on any system
system ! *user*	A specific user *user* on a specific system *system*
system ! `all`	All users on *system*
`all` ! *user*	A specific user *user* on all systems
`all`	All users on all systems

Users that have been given a limit cannot submit a print request with a higher priority level than the one assigned, nor can they increase the priority of a request already submitted. Any print requests submitted with priority levels higher than allowed will be given the highest priority allowed.

The third form of the command (with -u) removes any explicit priority level for the specified users. The fourth form of the command (with -q) sets the default highest priority level for all users who dont have a personal default priority. The last form of the command (with -l) lists the default priority level and the priority limits assigned to users.

8

Pre-Printed Forms

❑ **Overview**

A form is a sheet of paper, on which text or graphical displays have already been printed, that can be loaded into a local printer for use in place of plain stock. Common examples of forms include company letterhead, special paper stock, invoices, blank checks, vouchers, receipts, and labels.

Typically, several copies of a blank form are loaded into a printer, either as a tray of single sheets or as a box of fan-folded paper. The LP print service helps you manage the use of pre-printed forms, but does not provide any help in filling out a form. This is solely your application's responsibility. The print service keeps track of which print requests require special forms and which forms are currently mounted, and can alert you to the need to mount a new form.

This section tells you how you can manage the use of pre-printed forms with the LP print service. You will learn how to

▲ define a new form

▲ change the print service's description of an existing form

▲ remove the print service's description of a form

▲   examine the print service's description of a form

▲   restrict user access to a form

▲   restrict the form's availability to a subset of printers

▲   arrange alerting to the need to mount a form

▲   inform the print service that a form has been mounted

You can manage the use of pre-printed forms by menu or command. Selecting forms from the Printer Services menu, shown in Figure 8-1, invokes the Forms Management menu shown in Figure 8-2.

Figure 8-1: Managing Pre-printed Forms.
Choose forms *to define, modify, remove, and examine pre-printed forms.*

```
2   Line Printer Services Configuration and Operation
-----------------------------------------------------------
classes        - Manage Classes of Related Printers
filters        - Manage Filters for Special Processes
forms          - Manage Pre-printed Forms
operations     - Perform Daily Printer Service Operations
printers       - Configure Printers for the Printer Service
priorities     - Assign Print Queue Priorities to Users
requests       - Manage Active Print Requests
status         - Display Status of Printer Service
systems        - Configure Connection to Remote Systems
preSVR4        - Printer Setup
```

Figure 8-2: Forms Management Menu.
Choose the entry best suited to the task at hand.

```
3   Manage Pre-printed Forms
---------------------------------
add    - Add a New Form
list   - List Form Attributes
modify - Modify a Form
remove - Remove Forms
```

❑ Adding or Modifying a Form

When you want to provide a new form, you must define its characteristics. The print service will use this information for two purposes: to initialize the printer so that printing is done properly on the form, and to send you reminders about how to handle that form. Figure 8-3 describes the characteristics of a form and the default values for some of them.

Characteristic	Default	Description
Page length	66 lines	The length of the form, or of each page in a multi-page form. This can be expressed as the number of lines, or the size in inches or centimeters.
Page width	80 columns	The width of the form, expressed in characters, inches, or centimeters.
Number of pages	1 page	The number of pages in a multi-page form. The print service uses this number with a filter (if available) to restrict the alignment pattern to a length of one form. If no filter is available, the LP print service does not truncate the output.
Line pitch	6 lines/inch	A measure of how closely together separate lines appear on the form. It is specified as either lines per inch or lines per centimeter.
Character pitch	10 char/inch	A measure of how closely together separate characters appear on the form. It is specified as either characters per inch or characters per centimeter.
Character set choice	any	The character set, print wheel, or font cartridge that should be used when this form is used. A user may choose a different character set for his or her own print request when using this form, or you can insist that only one character set be used.
Ribbon color	any	If the form should always be printed using a certain color ribbon, then the LP print service can remind you which color to use when you mount the form.
Comment		Any remarks that might help users understand what the form is, when it should be used, and so on.

Figure 8-3: Characteristics of Pre-printed Forms.
The first nine characteristics define a form. You can also associate an alert command and allow and deny lists with the form.

Characteristic	Default	Description
Alignment pattern		A sample file that the LP print service uses to fill one blank form. When mounting the form, you can print this pattern on the form to align it properly. You can also define a content type for this pattern so that the printer service knows how to print it.
Alert command	none	You can arrange to be alerted when the number of requests waiting for the form or print wheel to be mounted has exceeded some threshold. The alert is a command, most likely a `mail` command or a command to `write` a message to your login terminal. The alert can be repeated every few minutes until the form is mounted, or given only once per form. You can also elect to receive no alerts, in which case you are responsible for checking to see if any print requests haven't printed because the proper form isn't mounted.
Users allowed Users denied		These are lists of users who are specifically denied or allowed use of the form. If the allow list is not empty, the deny list is ignored. If the allow list is empty, the deny list is used. If both lists are empty, there are no restrictions on who can use the form.

◆ *Note* The LP print service does not try to mask sensitive information in an alignment pattern. If you do not want sensitive information printed on sample forms (for instance, when you align checks) you should mask the appropriate data. The LP print service keeps the alignment pattern stored in a safe place, where only the user `lp` and the superuser `root` can read it.

When you've gathered this information about the form, enter it as input to the `lpforms` command. You may want to record this information first in a separate file so you can edit it before entering it with `lpforms`. You can then use the file as input instead of typing each piece of information separately after a prompt. Whichever method you use, enter the information in the following format:

```
Page length: scaled-number
Page width: scaled-number
Number of pages: integer
```

```
Line pitch: scaled-number
Character pitch: scaled-number
Character set choice: character-set-name[,mandatory]
Ribbon color: ribbon-color
Comment:
comment
Alignment pattern: [content-type]
alignment-pattern
```

Although these attributes are described in detail in Figure 8-3, a few points should be emphasized here. First, the phrase mandatory is optional and, if present, means that the user cannot override the character set choice in the form. Second, an optional *content-type* can be given with the alignment pattern. If this attribute is given, the print service uses it to determine, as necessary, how to filter and print the file.

With two exceptions, the information in the above list may appear in any order. The exceptions are the *alignment-pattern* (which must always appear last) and the *comment* (which must always follow the line with the Comment: prompt). If the *comment* contains a line beginning with a key phrase (such as Page length, Page width, and so on), precede that line with a > character so the key phrase is hidden. Be aware, though, that any initial > will be stripped from the comment when it is displayed.

Not all the information has to be given. When you don't specify values for the items listed Figure 8-3, the default values are used. To define the form, use one of the following commands

```
lpforms -f form-name -F file-name
lpforms -f form-name -
```

where *file-name* is the full path for the file.

The first command gets the form definition from a file; the second command gets the form definition from you, through the standard input. A *form-name* can be anything you choose, as long as it contains a maximum of fourteen alphanumeric characters and underscores.

If you need to change a form, just reenter one of the above commands. You need only provide information for items that must be changed; items for which you don't specify new information will stay the same.

❏ Using the Menu Interface to Add or Modify a Form

When you select add from the Forms Management menu shown in Figure 8-2, you fill out a short form giving the name of the new form or an already-existing form that you want to modify. The *form-name* contains 14 or fewer letters, digits, and underscores. If the form exists, its current characteristics are displayed (in a dialog box like the one shown in Figure 8-4) to serve as a model for the new form. You can edit some or all of the fields. If the form name is new, you will see the blank dialog box in Figure 8-4. When several forms are defined, repeatedly selecting (*choices*) cycles through the names of the available forms. Selecting (*save*) then displays the chosen model form.

Figure 8-4: Adding or Modifying a Form Description.
These characteristics define a pre-printed form. Most have default values: see Figure 8-3 for details.

```
4        Add/Modify Form <form-name>
-----------------------------------------------------
Page length:    Page width:
Line pitch:     Character pitch:
Number of Pages:
Character set choice:
Ribbon color:
Comment:

Alignment pattern file:

Alert command:

Number of requests:(Only appears if an alert command is supplied).
Frequency of alerts:(Only appears if an alert command is supplied.)

Users denied:
Users allowed:
```

❏ Removing a Form

The LP print service imposes no fixed limit on the number of forms you may define. It is a good idea, however, to remove forms that are no longer appropriate. If you don't, users will see a long list of obsolete forms when choosing a form, and may be confused. In addition, because the LP print service must occasionally look through all the forms listed before performing certain tasks, the failure to remove obsolete forms may require extra, unnecessary processing by the print service.

To remove a form, enter the following command:

```
lpforms -f form-name -x
```

or choose `remove` from the `Forms Management` menu, shown in Figure 8-2, and enter the *form-name*.

❏ Displaying a Form Description

You can examine a form definition once you've added it to the print service. There are two commands to use, depending on the information you want to examine. The `lpforms` command displays the form definition in a format suitable for re-input. The `lpstat` command displays the current status of the form.

```
lpforms -f form-name -l
lpforms -f form-name -l (optional) >file-name
lpstat -f form-name
lpstat -f form-name -l
```

The `lpforms` commands are restricted to the LP administrator (user `lp`) and the superuser `root` because they displays the alignment pattern, which may contain sensitive information. The `lpstat` commands can be used by anyone.

Choose `list` from the `Forms Management` menu shown in Figure 8-2 to display the definition of any or all forms in the system (the default *form-name* is `all`). The form characteristics are displayed in the same format as the dialog box of Figure 8-4.

❑ Restricting User Access to the Form

You can add names of users either to allow or to deny access using one of the following commands:

```
lpforms -f form-name -u allow:user-list
lpforms -f form-name -u deny:user-list
```

The *user-list* is a list of names of users separated by a comma or space. If you use spaces to separate the names, enclose the entire list (including the `allow:` or `deny:`) in quotes. Using `allow:all` allows everybody; using `deny:all` denies everybody.

To create allow and deny lists with the menu interface, choose `modify` from the `Forms Management` menu (Figure 8-2) and add the user names to the form's characteristics (Figure 8-4).

❑ Restricting the Form to a Subset of Printers

You can control the use of pre-printed forms on any printer, including remote printers. (Although you cannot mount forms on remote printers, your users may use forms on remote printers.) You may want to do this, for instance, if a printer is not well suited for printing on a particular form because of low print quality, or if the form cannot be lined up properly in the printer.

The LP print service will use a list of forms allowed or denied on a printer to warn you against mounting a form that is not allowed on the printer. However, you have the final word on this; the LP print service will not reject the mounting. The LP print service will, however, reject a user's request to print a file on a printer using a form not allowed on that printer. If, however, the printer is a local printer and the requested form is already mounted, the request will be printed on that form.

If you try to allow a form for a printer, but the printer does not have sufficient capabilities to handle the form, the command will be rejected.

The method of listing the forms allowed or denied for a printer is similar to the method used to list users allowed or denied access to the `cron` and `at` facilities. (See the description of the `crontab` command in the *UNIX System V Release 4 User's Reference Manual System Administrator's Reference Manual*.) Briefly, the rules are as follows:

▲ An *allow list* is a list of forms that are allowed to be used on the printer. A *deny list* is a list of forms that are not allowed to be used on the printer.

▲ If the allow list is not empty, only the forms listed are allowed; the deny list is ignored. If the allow list is empty, the forms listed in the deny list are not allowed. If both lists are empty, there are no restrictions on which forms may be used other than those restrictions that apply to a printer of a particular type, such as a PostScript printer for which a license is required.

▲ Specifying `all` in the allow list allows all forms; specifying `all` in the deny list denies all forms.

You can add names of forms to either list using one of the following commands:

```
lpadmin -p printer-name -f allow:form-list
lpadmin -p printer-name -f deny:form-list
```

The *form-list* is a comma or space separated list of names of forms. If you use spaces to separate names, enclose the entire list (including the `allow:` or `deny:` but not the `-f`) in quotes. See *More About lpadmin* in Chapter 3, *Configuring Printers*.

The first command shown above adds names to the allow list and removes them from the deny list. The second command adds names to the deny list and removes them from the allow list. To make the use of all forms permissible, specify `allow:all`; to deny permission for all forms, specify `deny:all`.

If you do not use this option, the LP print service will consider that the printer denies the use of all forms. It will, however, allow you to mount any form, thereby making it implicitly available to use.

❏ Alerting to Mount a Form

To arrange for alerting to the need to mount a form, enter one of the following commands:

```
lpforms -f form-name -A mail -Q integer -W minutes
lpforms -f form-name -A write -Q integer -W minutes
lpforms -f form-name -A 'command' -Q integer -W minutes
lpforms -f form-name -A none
```

The first two commands direct the print service to send you a mail message or write the message directly to your terminal. The third command asks the print service to run *command* for each alert. The fourth command above means do not send an alert when the form needs to be mounted. The number of requests that need to be waiting for the form is given as *integer* and *minutes* is the number of minutes between repeated alerts.

◆ *Note*   If you want mail sent or a message written to *another* person when a form is needed, use the third command listed; i.e., `-A 'mail user'` or `-A 'write user'`

Once you start receiving repeated alerts, you can direct the LP print service to stop sending you alerts for the current case only by giving the following command:

```
lpforms -f form-name -A quiet
```

Once the form has been mounted and unmounted again, alerts will start again if too many requests are waiting. Alerts also start again if the number of requests waiting falls below the -Q threshold and then rises up to the -Q threshold again, as when waiting requests are canceled or if the type of alerting is changed.

If *form-name* is all in any of the commands above, the alerting condition will apply to all forms.

To specify alert handling with the menu interface, choose modify from the Forms Management menu (Figure 8-2) and add the alert command and its parameters to the form's characteristics (Figure 8-4).

❑ Mounting a Form

Before the LP print service can start printing files that need a pre-printed form, you must physically mount the form on a printer, and notify the LP print service that you have mounted it. (It is not necessary that a form be included on the allow list to mount it.) If alerting has been set on the form or print wheel, you will be alerted when enough print requests are queued waiting for it to be mounted.

When you mount a form you may want to see if it is lined up properly. If an alignment pattern has been defined for the form, you can ask that this be repeatedly printed after you've mounted the form, until you have adjusted the printer so that the alignment is correct.

Mounting a form or print wheel involves first loading it onto the printer and then telling the LP print service that it is mounted. Because it is difficult to do this on a printer that's currently printing, and because the LP print service will continue to print files not needing the form on the printer, you will probably have to disable the printer first. Thus, the proper procedure is to follow these three steps:

1. Disable the printer, using the `disable` command.

2. Mount the new form as described below.

3. Re-enable the printer, using the `enable` command. (The `disable` and `enable` commands are described in the *Enabling and Disabling a Printer* section of Chapter 6.)

First, physically load the new form into the printer. Then enter the following command to tell the LP print service it has been mounted.

```
lpadmin -p printer-name -M -f form-name -a -o filebreak
```

If you are mounting a form with an alignment pattern defined for it, you will be asked to press the ⟨ *return* ⟩ key before each copy of the alignment pattern is printed. After the pattern is printed, you can adjust the printer and press the ⟨ *return* ⟩ key again. If no alignment pattern has been defined, you won't be asked to press the ⟨ *return* ⟩ key. You can drop the `-a` and `-o filebreak` options if you don't want to bother with the alignment pattern.

The `-o filebreak` option tells the LP print service to add a formfeed after each copy of the alignment pattern. The actual control sequence used for the formfeed depends on the printer involved and is obtained from the `terminfo` database. If the alignment pattern already includes a formfeed, leave out the `-o filebreak` option.

If you want to dismount a form or print wheel, use the following command:

```
lpadmin -p printer-name -M -f none
```

Print requests that require a particular form will be held in a queue until the form is mounted. Until you've mounted a form on a printer, only print requests that don't require a form will be printed.

❑ More About `lpforms`

In the preceding sections, the options and uses for the `lpforms` are given as each administrative task is presented. In this section, all the information about `lpforms` is collected together; use it as a reference as you provide pre-printed forms to your users.

The `lpforms` command is used to administer the use of preprinted forms, such as company letterhead paper, with the LP print service. A form is speci-fied by its *form-name*. Users may specify a form when submitting a print request [see `lp` (1)]. The argument `all` can be used instead of *form-name* with either of the command lines shown below.

    lpforms -f *form-name options*

    lpforms -f *form-name* -A *alert-type* [-Q *minutes*] [-W *requests*]

The first command line allows the administrator to add, change, and delete forms, to list the attributes of an existing form, and to allow and deny users access to particular forms. The second command line is used to establish the method by which the administrator is alerted that the form *form-name* must be mounted on a printer.

With the first `lpforms` command line, one of the following options must be used:

Option	Meaning and Use
-F *pathname*	To add or change form *form-name*, as specified by the infor-mation in *pathname*.
-	To add or change form *form-name*, as specified by the infor-mation from standard input.
-x	To delete form *form-name*. This option cannot by used with any other option.
-l	To list the attributes of form *form-name*

Figure 8-5:
Options to the
`lpforms` *Com-*
mand.
These are the
options for the
`lpforms` *com-*
mand. All of them
assume the pres-
ence of `-f` ***form-***
name.

Adding or Changing a Form

The -F *pathname* option is used to add a new form, *form-name*, to the LP print service, or to change the attributes of an existing form. The form description is taken from *pathname* if the -F option is given, or from the standard input if the - option is used. One of these two options must be used to define or change a form. *pathname* is the path name of a file that contains all or any subset of the following information about the form.

```
Page length: scaled-decimal-number
Page width: scaled-decimal-number
Number of pages: integer
Line pitch: scaled-decimal-number
Character pitch: scaled-decimal-number
Character set choice: character-set-or- print-wheel [ mandatory ]
Ribbon color: ribbon-color
Comment:
comment
Alignment pattern: [ content-type ]
alignment-pattern
```

The term *scaled-decimal-number* refers to a non-negative number used to indicate a unit of size. The unit is shown by a trailing letter attached to the number. Three types of scaled decimal numbers can be used with the LP print service: numbers that show sizes in centimeters (marked with a trailing c), numbers that show sizes in inches (marked with a trailing i), and numbers that show sizes in units appropriate to use (without a trailing letter), that is, lines, characters, lines per inch, or characters per inch.

Except for the last two lines, the above lines may appear in any order. The Comment: and *comment* items must appear in consecutive order but may appear before the other items, and the Alignment pattern: and the *alignment-pattern* items must appear in consecutive order at the end of the file. Also, the *comment* item may not contain a line that begins with any of the key phrases above, unless the key phrase is preceded with a > character. Any leading > found in the *comment* will be removed when the comment is displayed. Case distinctions in the key phrases are ignored.

When this command is issued, the form specified by *form-name* is added to the list of forms. If the form already exists, its description is changed to reflect the new information. Once added, a form is available for use in a print request, except where access to the form has been restricted, as described under the -u option. A form may also be allowed to be used on certain printers only.

See Figure 8-3 at the beginning of this chapter for a detailed description of the form characteristics and the default values that will be used if none are specified.

Deleting a Form:

The -x option is used to delete the form *form-name* from the LP print service.

Listing Form Attributes

The -l option is used to list the attributes of the existing form *form-name*. The attributes listed are those described under *Adding and Changing a Form* above. Because of the potentially sensitive nature of the alignment pattern, only the administrator can examine the form with this command. Other people may use the lpstat command to examine the non-sensitive part of the form description.

Allowing and Denying Access to a Form

The -u option, followed by allow:*user-list* or deny:*userlist* lets you determine which users will be allowed to specify a particular form with a print request. This option can be used with the -F or - option, each of which is described above under *Adding or Changing a Form*.

The *user-list* argument may include any or all of the following constructs:

*Figure 8-6: Lim-
iting User
Access to Forms.*
*The allow and
deny lists contain
entries of the form
shown in the first
column.*

user-list Item	Meaning
user	*user* on any system
`all`	all users on all systems
local-system ! *user*	*user* on *local-system* only
! *user*	*user* on local system only
`all` ! *user*	*user* on any system
`all!all`	all users on all systems
system ! `all`	all users on *system*
`!all`	all users on local system

The LP print service keeps two lists of users for each form: an *allow-list* of peo-ple allowed to use the form, and a *deny-list* of people that may not use the form. The `-u allow:`*user-list* option adds users to the allow list and removes them from the deny list while the `-u deny:`*user-list* option adds users to the deny list and removes them from the allow list. (Both forms of the `-u` option can be used with either the `-F` or the `-` option.)

If the allow-list is not empty, only the users in the list are allowed access to the form, regardless of the contents of the deny-list. If the allow-list is empty but the deny-list is not, the users in the deny-list may not use the form, (but all others may use it). All users can be denied access to a form by specifying `-f deny:all`. All users can be allowed access to a form by specifying `-f allow:all` (the default).

Setting an Alert to Mount a Form

The `-f` *form-name* option is used with `-A` *alert-type* to define an alert to mount the form when there are queued jobs that need it. If `-A` is not specified, no alert will be sent for form *form-name*. The method by which the alert is sent depends on the value of the *alert-type* argument, shown in Figure 8-7.

Value	Description
`mail`	Send the alert message by electronic mail to the administrator.
`write`	Write the message to the terminal on which the administrator is logged in. If the administrator is logged in on several terminals, one is chosen arbitrarily.
`quiet`	Do not send messages for the current condition. An administrator can use this option to stop receiving messages about a known problem. Once the fault has been cleared and printing resumes, alert messages will be sent when another fault occurs.
`none`	Do not send messages; any existing alert definition for the printer will be removed. No alert will be sent when the printer faults until a different alert-type (except `quiet`) is used.
`shell-command`	Run the shell-command each time the alert needs to be sent. The shell command should expect the message in standard input. If there are blanks embedded in the command, enclose the command in quotes. Note that the `mail` and `write` values for this option are equivalent to the values `mail` *user-name* and `write` *user-name* respectively, where *user-name* is the current name for the administrator. This will be the login name of the person submitting this command unless he or she has used the `su` command to change to another user ID. If the `su` command has been used to change the user ID, then the *user-name* for the new ID is used.
`list`	Display the type of the alert for the printer fault. No change is made to the alert.

Figure 8-7: Possible Values for alert-type. You can specify what the print service will do when a form mount request occurs.

The message sent appears as follows:

```
The form form-name needs to be mounted
on the printer(s):
printer₁ (integer₁ requests).
integerₙ print requests await this form.
Use the ribbon-color ribbon.
Use the print-wheel print wheel, if appropriate.
```

The printers listed are those that the administrator had earlier specified were candidates for this form. The number $integer_i$ listed next to each $printer_i$ is the number of requests eligible for the printer. The number $integer_n$ shown after the list of printers is the total number of requests awaiting the form. It will be less than the sum of the other numbers if some requests can be handled by more than one printer. The *ribbon-color* and *print-wheel* are those specified in the form description. The last line in the message is always sent, even if none of the printers listed use print wheels, because the administrator may choose to mount the form on a printer that does use a print wheel.

Where any color ribbon or any print wheel can be used, the statements above will read:

```
Use any ribbon.
Use any print-wheel.
```

If *form-name* is any, the alerting defined in this command applies to any form for which an alert has not yet been defined. If *form-name* is all, the alerting defined in this command applies to all forms.

If the -W option is not given, the default procedure is that only one message will be sent per need to mount the form. Not specifying the -W option is equivalent to specifying -W once or -W 0. If *minutes* is a number greater than 0, an alert will be sent at intervals specified by *minutes*.

If the -Q option is also given, the alert will be sent when a certain number (specified by the argument *requests*) of print requests that need the form are waiting. If the -Q option is not given, or the value of *requests* is 1 or any (which are both the default), a message is sent as soon as anyone submits a print request for the form when it is not mounted.

Listing the Current Alert

The -f option, followed by -A list is used to list the type of alert that has been defined for the specified form *form-name*. No change is made to the alert. If form-name is recognized by the print service, one of the following lines is sent to the standard output, depending on the type of alert for the form.

- When *requests* requests are queued:
  alert with *shell-command* every *minutes* minutes

- When *requests* requests are queued:
  write to *user-name* every *minutes* minutes

- When *requests* requests are queued:
  mail to *user-name* every *minutes* minutes

- No alert

The phrase `every` *minutes* `minutes` is replaced with `once` if *minutes* (`-W` *minutes*) is 0.

Terminating an Active Alert

The `-A quiet` option is used to stop messages for the current condition. An administrator can use this option to temporarily stop receiving further messages about a known problem. Once the form has been mounted and then unmounted, messages will again be sent when the number of print requests reaches the threshold *requests*.

Removing an Alert Definition

No messages will be sent after the `-A none` option is used until the `-A` option is given again with a different *alert-type*. This can be used to stop further messages from being sent (permanently!) since the existing alert definition for the form is removed.

9

Filters

❑ Overview

A *filter* provides three related functions:

▲ It converts the files in a print request into a data stream that will print properly on a given printer.

▲ It handles the various print modes offered by the `-y` option to `lp`, such as two-sided printing, landscape-mode printing, draft or letter quality output, etc.

▲ It detects printer faults and informs the print service so that it can send an alert.

Not every filter will provide all three functions. However, given the printer-specific nature of these tasks, the print service has been designed so that you, the printer manufacturer, or third-party software supplier can provide modular filters that can easily be incorporated into the print service.

A default filter is provided with the LP print service to handle simple fault detection; it does not convert files nor supply the special print modes.

This chapter starts with a closer look at the three tasks that a filter may perform, and then describes the procedures for defining, modifying, removing, examining, and writing a filter.

❏ File Conversion

The LP print service allows you to assign a *type* to each printer you add to the system and allows a user to assign a *type* to each file submitted for printing. This information is used to match a file with the printer that will best reproduce the file. Since many applications can generate data for various printers, this is often sufficient.

Chances are, however, that not all the applications you support will produce output your printers can print. By defining and creating a filter that will convert such output into a format that your printer can handle, you can begin to offer printing services to a larger set of applications and users.

Each filter that is added to the system is typed as well, defining the input types it can accept and the output types it can produce. If the print service cannot match a file type to a printer type, it consults the table of filters to find one that will do the conversion.

Example - No Data Conversion Required

A spreadsheet program can generate output in several different formats, including a format that is supported directly by a printer on the system. No filter is necessary if the user directs the spreadsheet application to produce output for that printer.

Example- Converting troff into postscript

A user has run the `troff` word processing program to produce a copy of a large document. The output has content type `troff`, but the printer takes `simple` and `postscript` files. The print service has a filter that converts `troff` to `postscript`, so the user will get pretty output.

❑ Special Print Modes

Each filter you add to the filter table can be registered as handling:

```
Input type
Output type
Printer type
Character pitch
Line pitch
Page length
Page width
Pages to print
Character set
Form name
Number of copies
Modes
```

The print service provides a default handling for all of these properties except `Modes`. However, it may be more efficient to have a filter handle some of them, or it may be that a filter has to understand several of the properties at once to do a proper job of printing the job. For example, a filter may need to know the page size, line pitch, and character pitch if it is going to break up the pages in a file to fit on printed pages. Or perhaps a function like making multiple copies can be handled most efficiently by the printer. A filter can be used to bypass the print service's default handling of multiple copies requests. Additional filters are required to handle variations in output modes such as two-sided printing, landscape printing, draft or letter quality printing.

❑ Printer Fault Handling

Just as file format conversion and special printing modes are printer-specific, so is detecting printer faults. The print service provides a general fault detection mechanism that will work for most printers. However, it is limited to checking for "hang-ups" (loss of carrier or the printer going off-line) and excessive delays in printing (an XOFF with no matching XON, for instance). It also can't determine the cause of a fault, so it can't tell you what to look for.

A properly designed filter can provide better, printer-specific, fault coverage. Some printers are able to send a message to the host describing the reason for the fault. Others indicate a fault by a different mechanism than dropping carrier or shutting off the data flow. A filter can improve printer service by giving you more information about a fault and by detecting more of them.

The print service has a simple interface that lets the filters get fault information to you. The interface program that manages the filters takes all error messages from the filters and places them into an alert message that will be sent to you according to the alerting method you defined (see *Catching Printer Fault Alerts* in Chapter 3). If you set the printer configuration so that printing should automatically resume after a fault is cleared, the interface program will keep the filter active so that it can pick right up where it left off.

❏ Guidelines for Filters

Here are guidelines that will help you choose a good filter:

1. Examine the kinds of files people submit for printing that will have to be processed by the filter. If they stand alone, that is, if they do not reference other files that the filter will need, the filter is probably okay. Check also to see if the filter expects any other files except those submitted by a user for printing.

2. If there can be referenced files inside the files submitted for printing or if the filter will need files other than those submitted by a user, then the filter is likely to fail because it will not be able to access the additional files. Don't use the program as a filter; have each user run the program before submitting the files for printing.

Referenced files that are always given with full path names *may* be okay but only if the filter is used for local print requests. When used on requests submitted from a remote machine for printing on your machine, the filter may still fail if the referenced files are only on the remote machine.

❑ Defining a Filter

There are several properties of the filter that you must describe for the print service:

▲ Input types

This is the list of file types that the filter can process. The file type name can be up to 14 characters (including dashes, but not under-scores). The default type is `simple`. Most filters can take only one input type, but the print service doesn't restrict them to one. Several file types may be similar enough that one filter can handle them all. If more than one filter can accept the same input type, use the same input-type name each time.

These names should be advertised to your users so they know how to name their file's type when they submit the file for printing.

▲ Output types

This is the list of file types that the filter can produce as output. For each file, the filter produces a single output type but it may be able to vary that type on demand. The names of the output types are also restricted to 14 letters, digits, and dashes.

The output type names should either match the types of printers you have on your system or should match the input types handled by other filters. The LP print service will connect filters together in a shell pipeline to produce a new filter if it finds that several passes by different filters are needed to convert a file. It's unlikely that you will need this level of sophistication, but the print service allows it. The default type is `simple`.

▲ Printer types

This is a list of printer types for which the filter can convert files. For most filters this list will be identical to the output types, but it can be different. For most printers, you can leave this part of the filter defini-tion blank.

▲ Printers

A filter should be able to work with all printers that accept the output that the filter produces. However, you may have some printers that, although they're of the correct type for a filter, are in other ways not adequate for the output that the filter will produce. For instance, you may want to dedicate one printer for fast turn-around; only files that the printer can handle without filtering will be sent to that printer. You may designate other printers of identical type to be used for files that may need extensive filtering before they can be printed. You'll label the filter as working with only the latter printers.

▲ Filter Type

The LP print service recognizes "fast" filters and "slow" filters. Fast filters are labeled "fast" either because they incur little overhead in preparing a file for printing or because they must have access to the printer when they run. Filters that detect printer faults, for instance, are always fast filters. Filters that incur a lot of overhead in preparing a file and that don't have to have access to the printer should be labeled "slow." The print service runs slow filters in the background without tying up a printer.

▲ Command

This is the full path name of the filter program to run. If there are any fixed options that the program will always need, you can include them here.

▲ Options

The printing modes and options, like the page length, a list of pages to print, the number of copies, and portrait or landscape orientation, are passed to the filter by converting the lp options into filter options. Templates of the form

keyword pattern = replacement

indicate the transformations. These templates are described in more detail in the **Templates** section below.

To define a filter, gather this information about the filter then either enter it in a file or type it directly as input to the lpfilter command. Present the information as it is listed below:

```
Input types: input-type-list
Output types: output-type-list
Printer types: printer-type-list
Printers: printer-list
Filter type: fast or slow
Command: pathname [options ]
Options: template-list
```

When you enter a list, separate the items in the list with blanks or commas. Missing information is assigned the defaults described above and shown in Figure 9-5. Once you have a filter definition complete, enter one of the following commands to add the filter to the system:

```
lpfilter -f filter-name -F file-name
lpfilter -f filter-name -
```

The first command gets the filter definition from a file, and the second command gets the filter definition interactively.

Templates

The *templates-list* is a list of templates separated by commas and has the following form:

keyword   pattern=replacement

The *keyword* identifies the particular printing characteristic that will be addressed in the template. The *pattern* is either a value of the characteristic or an asterisk (*) that stands as a place-holder for any value. Figure 9-1 shows keywords and patterns that correspond to the various data the filter can specify or access.

▲ The values of the INPUT and OUTPUT templates come from the file type that needs to be converted by the filter and the output type that has to be produced, respectively. They'll each be a type registered with the filter.

▲ The value for the TERM template is the printer type.

▲ The values for the CPI, LPI, LENGTH, and WIDTH templates come from the user's request, the form being used, or the defaults for the printer.

▲ The value for the PAGES template is a list of pages that should be printed. Typically it is a list of page ranges, either a pair of numbers or a single number, each range separated by a comma (e.g., 1-5, 6, 8, 10 for pages 1 through 5, 6, 8, and 10). However, whatever value was given in the -P option to a print request is passed unchanged.

▲ The value for the CHARSET template is the name of the character set to be used.

▲ The value for the FORM template is the name of the form being printed on, if any.

▲ The value of the COPIES template is the number of copies of the file that should be made. If the filter uses this template, LP will reduce the number of copies of the filtered file it will print to 1 since this "single copy" will really be the multiple copies produced by the filter.

▲ The value of the MODES template comes from the -y option of the lp command, the command a person uses to submit a print request. Since a user can give several -y options, there may be several values for the MODES template. The values will be applied in the left-to-right order given by the user.

Figure 9-1: Template Keywords and Patterns. Here is the correspondence between filter specifications and template specifications.

Characteristic	Keyword	Possible *patterns*
Input type	INPUT	*content-type*
Output type	OUTPUT	*content-type*
Printer type	TERM	*printer-type*
Character pitch	CPI	*integer*
Line pitch	LPI	*integer*
Page length	LENGTH	*integer*
Page width	WIDTH	*integer*
Pages to print	PAGES	*page-list*
Character set	CHARSET	*character-set*
Form name	FORM	*form-name*
Number of copies	COPIES	*integer*
Modes	MODES	*mode*

The replacement shows how the value of a template should be given to the filter program. It is typically a literal option, sometimes with the placeholder * included to show where the value goes.

Example - Defining a New Filter that Uses Standard Print Options

The filter program is called `/usr/bin/npf`. It takes two input types, `nroff37` and `X`, produces an output type called `TX`, and will work with any printer of type `TX`, The program accepts three options:

`-Xb`	only for the input type X
`-l` *integer*	for the length of the output page
`-w` *integer*	for the width of the output page

The filter definition would look like this:

```
Input types: X,nroff37
Output types: TX
Printer types: TX
Command: /usr/bin/npf
Options: INPUT X = -Xb, LENGTH * = -l*,
WIDTH * = -w*
```

If a user submits a file of type `nroff37` and asks that it be printed by a printer named `laser1` of type `TX`, and requests a page length of `72`,

```
lp -T nroff37 -d laser1 -o length=72
```

then this filter will be called upon by the print service to convert the file. The filter will be invoked as

```
/usr/bin/npf -l72
```

Another user submits a file of type `X` that is to be printed on the same printer, with default length and width. The filter will be invoked as

```
/usr/bin/npf -Xb
```

Example- Defining a New Filter with Custom Options

The filter program is called `/usr/bin/x9700`. It takes one input type, `troff`, produces an output type called `9700` and will work with any printer of type `9700`. The program has one fixed option, `-ib`, and accepts three other options:

`-l` *integer*	for the length of the output page
`-s` *name*	for the character set
`-o` `portrait` *or* `-o` `landscape`	for portrait or landscape orientation of the paper

You've decided that your users need give just the abbreviations `port` and `land` when they ask for the paper orientation. Since these are not options intrinsic to the print service, users will specify them using the `-y` option to the `lp` command.

The filter definition would look like this:

```
Input types: troff
Output types: 9700
Printer types: 9700
Command: /usr/bin/x9700 -ib
Options: LENGTH * = -l *,
         CHARSET * = -s *,
         MODES port = -o portrait,
         MODES land = -o landscape
```

(The `Options:` line is split into several lines for readability; you would enter it as a single line.)

If a user submits a file of type `troff` for printing on a printer of type `9700` and requests landscape orientation using the `gothic` character set,

```
lp -T troff -S gothic -y land
```

then this filter will be invoked by the print service to convert the file as follows:

```
/usr/bin/x9700 -ib -s gothic -o landscape
```

◆ *Note* If a pattern or replacement must include a comma or equals sign (=), escape its special meaning by preceding it with a backslash. A backslash in front of these two characters will be removed when the pattern or replacement is used. (All other backslashes are left alone.)

Example- Using Templates to Convert Options

The template

```
MODES landscape = -l
```

shows that if a print request is submitted with the `-y landscape` option, the filter will be given the option `-l`.

Example- Using Templates for Printer Type Conversion

The template

```
TERM * = \-T *
```

shows that the filter will be given the option `-T` *printer-type* for whichever *printer-type* is associated with a print request using the filter.

Example- Using the MODES Template

Consider the template

```
MODES prwidth\=\(.*\) = \-w\1
```

Suppose a user gives the command

```
lp -y prwidth=10
```

From the table above, the print service determines that the -y option is handled by a MODES template. The MODES template here works because the *pattern* prwidth\=\(.*\) matches the prwidth=10 given by the user. The *replacement* -w\1 causes the print service to generate the filter option -w 10.

Defining a Filter with Menus

When you select filters from the Printer Services menu, as shown in Figure 9-2, the Filter Management menu is invoked (shown in Figure 9-3). Choose add to produce the first of two dialog boxes that will walk you through the process of defining the filter.

 The system comes with a number of built-in filters. When the first dialog box is displayed, press (*choices*) for a list of possible filters. You can either select one from the list or you can exit the list, type in the filter name, and press (*save*).   The dialog box shown in Figure 9-4 results, with the default settings for that filter already entered. You can then modify those settings to describe your own filter, or you can activate one of the built-in ones. Your response to New Filter: is the name you will use to reference the filter from this point on.

```
2 Line Printer Services Configuration and Operation
----------------------------------------------------------
classes         - Manage Classes of Related Printers
filters         - Manage Filters for Special Processes
forms           - Manage Pre-printed Forms
operations      - Perform Daily Printer Service Operations
printers        - Configure Printers for the Printer Service
priorities      - Assign Print Queue Priorities to Users
requests        - Manage Active Print Requests
status          - Display Status of Printer Service
systems         - Configure Connection to Remote Systems
preSVR4         - Printer Setup
```

Figure 9-2: Managing Filters.
Choose `filters` *to define, modify, remove, and examine pre-printed forms.*

```
3 Manage Filters for Special Processing
-------------------------------------------
add      - Add a New Filter
list     - Display Filter Information
modify   - Modify Filters
remove   - Remove Filters
restore  - Restore Filters to Factory Settings
```

Figure 9-3: Filter Management Menu.
Choose the entry best suited to the task at hand.

```
5   Add/Modify Filter <filter-name>
-------------------------------------------
Input types:     simple
Output types:    simple
Printer types:   any
Printers:        any

Fast or slow filter: slow

Filter command:

New filter options? Yes
```

Figure 9-4: Dialog Box for Setting Filter Specifications.
Fill in the fields that you want to add or change. The default values are shown in boldface type.

❑ Displaying a Filter

The `lpfilter` command displays the definition of the filter in a form suitable to be input so that you can direct the output to a file for future reference. The command is:

    lpfilter -f *filter-name* -l >*file-name*

Without the optional *file-name*, the output will be printed on the standard output device.

In the menu interface, select `list` from the `Filter Management` menu shown in Figure 9-3. You will be prompted for the name of the filter.

❑ Modifying a Filter

To modify a filter you can

▲ create a file with just the changes in it, in the same format as described for defining a filter, and use the `-F` option to `lpfilter` to record the changes, or

▲ use the `-l` option of `lpfilter`, as shown above, to generate a file containing the current specifications, edit that file to reflect the changes, and then use the `-F` option to `lpfilter` to record the changes, or

▲ type the changes as standard input to `lpfilter`.

To modify a filter by menu, select `modify` from the `Filter Management` menu shown in Figure 9-3 and enter the name of the filter to be modified. You can enter (choices) to select from the list of possible filters. Once the filter is named, the dialog box shown in Figure 9-4 is displayed and you are free to change any entry.

❑ Removing a Filter

To remove a filter, type the following:

```
lpfilter -f filter-name -x
```

To remove a filter by menu, select `remove` in the `Filter Management` menu (Figure 9-3) and enter the name of the filter.

▼ *Caution*   Adding, changing, or deleting filters can cause queued print requests to be canceled. Because of this possibility, you may want to make changes to filters during periods when the print service is not very busy.

❑ Writing a Filter

A filter is used by the LP print service each time it has to print a type of file that isn't acceptable by a printer. A filter can be as simple or as complex as needed; there are only a few external requirements:

▲ The filter should get the content of a user's file from its standard input and send the converted file to the standard output.

▲ A `slow` filter can send error messages to standard error. They will be collected and sent to the user who submitted the file for printing. A `fast` filter sends errors to the standard output where they can be read by the user.

▲ If a `slow` filter dies when receiving a signal, the print request is stopped and the user who submitted the request is notified. Likewise, if a `slow` filter exits with a non-zero exit code, the print request is stopped and the user is notified. A `fast` filter should exit with a non-zero exit code *only* if a printer fault has prevented it from finishing the printing of a file.

▲ A filter should not depend on other files that normally would not be accessible to a regular user; if a filter fails when run directly by a user, it will fail when run by the LP print service.

If you want your filter to detect printer faults, you must also fulfill the following requirements:

▲ If possible, the filter should wait for a fault to be cleared before exiting. Additionally, it should continue printing at the top of the page where printing stopped after the fault clears. If the administrator does not want this contingency followed, the LP print service will stop the filter before alerting the administrator.

▲ It should send printer fault messages to its standard error as soon as the fault is recognized. It does not have to exit, but can wait as described above.

▲ It should *not* send messages about errors in the file to standard error. These should be included in the standard output stream, where they can be read by the user.

▲ It should exit with a zero exit code if the user's file is finished (even if errors in the file have prevented it from being printed correctly).

▲ It should exit with a non-zero exit code *only* if a printer fault has prevented it from finishing a file.

▲ When added to the filter table, it must be added as a `fast` filter. (See the *Defining a Filter* section in this chapter for details.)

❑ More About `lpfilter`

The `lpfilter` command is used to add, change, delete, and list a filter used with the LP print service. These filters are used to convert the content type of a file to a content type acceptable to a printer. In the preceding sections of this chapter, the various `lpfilter` functions have been presented in a task-oriented way. In this section, the command options drive the discussion, making the section a useful reference.

The legal forms of the command are:

```
lpfilter -f filter-name -F path-name
lpfilter -f filter-name -
lpfilter -f filter-name -i
lpfilter -f filter-name -x
lpfilter -f filter-name -l
```

One of the following options must be used with the `lpfilter` command:

▲   `-F` *path-name* or `-` (for standard input) to add or change a filter

▲   `-i` to reset an original filter to its factory setting

▲   `-x` to delete a filter, or

▲   `-l` to list a filter description.

The argument `all` can be used instead of a *filter-name* with any of these options. When `all` is specified with the `-F` or `-` option, the requested change is made to all filters. Using `all` with the `-i` option has the effect of restoring to their original settings all filters for which predefined settings were initially available. Using the `all` argument with the `-x` option results in all filters being deleted, and using it with the `-l` option produces a list of all filters.

Adding or Changing a Filter

The filter named in the `-f` option is added to the filter table. If the filter already exists, its description is changed to reflect the new information in the input.

The filter description is taken from the *path-name* if the `-F` option is given, or from the standard input if the `-` option is given. One of the two must be given to define or change a filter. If the filter named is one originally delivered with the LP print service, the `-i` option will restore the original filter description.

When an existing filter is changed with the `-F` or `-` option, items that are not specified in the new information are left as they were. When a new filter is added with this command, unspecified items are given default values.

Filters are used to convert the content of a request into a data stream acceptable to a printer. For a given print request, the LP print service will know the following:

▲   the type of content in the request,

▲   the name of the printer,

▲   the type of the printer,

▲   the types of content acceptable to the printer, and

▲ the modes of printing asked for by the originator of the request.

It will use this information to find a filter or a pipeline of filters that will convert the content into a type acceptable to the printer.

The list of items that provide input to this command is shown below. Figure 9-5 gives a description of each item and the print service defaults that will be used if you don't provide a value. All lists are comma or space separated.

```
Input types: content-type-list
Output types: content-type-list
Printer types: printer-type-list
Printers: printer-list
Filter type: filter-type
Command: shell-command
Options: template-list
```

Templates

Each template has the following form:

keyword pattern = replacement

The *keyword* names the characteristic that the template attempts to map into a filter specific option; each valid *keyword* is listed in Figure 9-6. A *pattern* is one of the following:

▲ a literal pattern of one of the forms listed in the table,

▲ a single asterisk (*), or

▲ a regular expression.

If *pattern* matches the value of the characteristic, the template fits and is used to generate a filter specific option. The *replacement* is what will be used as the option.

Item	Default	Meaning and Use
Input types	simple	This gives the types of content that can be accepted by the filter.
Output types	simple	This gives the types of content that the filter can produce from any of the input content types.
Printer types	any	This gives the *types* of printers for which the filter can be used. The print service will restrict the use of the filter to these types of printers.
Printers	any	This gives the *names* of the printers for which the filter can be used. The print service will restrict the use of the filter to just the printers named.
Filter types	slow	This marks the filter as a slow filter or a fast filter. Slow filters are generally those that take a long time to convert their input. The print service will run slow filters without attaching a printer to their standard output, to allow the printer to work on other requests while the filter converts the data. Filters for remote printers must be marked slow. Fast filters are those that convert their input quickly, or those that must be connected to the printer when run (e.g., ones that handle printer faults).
Command		This specifies the command to invoke the filter. The full program pathname as well as fixed options must be included in the *shell-command*. Additional options are constructed based on the characteristics of each print request and on the Options field. A command must be given for each filter. It must accept a data stream as standard input and produce the converted data stream on its standard output.
Options		This is a comma separated list of templates used by the print service to construct options to the filter from the characteristics of each print request listed in Figure 9-6.

Figure 9-5: Characteristics of a Filter.
These characteristics define a filter. They help the print service choose the appropriate filter for each print request.

Regular expressions are the same as those found in the ed(1) or vi(1) commands. This includes the \(...\) and \n constructions, which can be used to extract portions of the *pattern* for copying into the *replacement*, and the &, which can be used to copy the entire *pattern* into the *replacement*.

The *replacement* can also contain a *. It will be replaced with the entire *pattern*, just like the & of ed(1).

Figure 9-6: Filter Options.
Here are the keywords and patterns used to rewrite a filter command for a particular print request and their correspondence to lp options.

lp Option	Characteristic	Keyword	Possible *patterns*
-T	Input type Output type Printer type	INPUT OUTPUT TERM	*content-type* *content-type* *content-type*
-d	Printer name	PRINTER	*printer-name*
-o cpi=	Character pitch	CPI	*integer*
-o lpi=	Line pitch	LPI	*integer*
-o length=	Page length	LENGTH	*integer*
-o width=	Page width	WIDTH	*integer*
-P	Pages to print	PAGES	*page-list*
-S	Character set Print wheel	CHARSET CHARSET	*character-set-name* *print-wheel-name*
-f	Form Name	FORM	*form-name*
-y	Modes	MODES	*mode*
-n	Number of copies	COPIES	*integer*

If necessary, the print service will construct a filter pipeline by concatenating several filters to handle the user's file and all the print options. If the print service constructs a filter pipeline, the INPUT and OUTPUT values used for each filter in the pipeline are the types of the input and output for that filter, not for the entire pipeline.

Deleting a Filter

The -x option is used to delete the filter specified in *filter-name* from the filter table.

Listing a Filter Description

The `-l` option is used to list the description of the filter named in *filter-name*. If the command is successful, the following message is sent to standard output:

```
Input types: content-type-list
Output types: content-type-list
Printer types: printer-type-list
Printers: printer-list
Filter type: filter-type
Command: shell-command
Options: template-list
```

If the command fails, an error message is sent to standard error.

10

PostScript Printers

❏ Overview

PostScript is a general purpose programming language, like C or Pascal. In addition to providing the usual features of a language, however, PostScript allows a programmer to specify the appearance of both text and graphics on a page.

A PostScript printer is a printer equipped with a computer that runs an interpreter for processing PostScript language files. When a PostScript printer receives a file, it interprets and then prints it. Unless special provisions have been made by the manufacturer, files submitted to a PostScript printer must be written in the PostScript language.

Why would you want to use a PostScript printer? PostScript provides excellent facilities for managing text and graphics and combining them. Graphics operators facilitate the construction of geometric figures that can then be positioned and scaled with any orientation. The text capabilities allow the user to specify a number of different fonts that can be placed on a page in any position, size, or orientation. Because text is treated as graphics, text and graphics are readily combined. Moreover, the language is resolution and device independent, so that draft copies can be proofed on a low-resolution device and the final version printed in higher resolution on a different device.

Applications that support PostScript, including word-processing and publishing software, will create documents in the PostScript language without intervention by the user. Thus, it is not necessary to know the details of the language to take advantage of its features. However, standard files that many applications produce cannot be printed on a PostScript printer because they are not described in the language. The LP print service provides optional filters to convert many of these files to PostScript so that users may take advantage of PostScript and continue to use their standard applications, such as `troff`.

❏ How to Use a PostScript Printer

When the PostScript printers and filters have been installed, the print service manages PostScript files like any others. If `psfile` is a file containing a PostScript document and `psprinter` has been defined to as a PostScript printer, the command

```
lp -d psprinter -T postscript psfile
```

will schedule the print request and manage the transmission of the request to the PostScript printer.

❏ Support of Non-PostScript Print Requests

Because PostScript is a language and PostScript printers are expecting print requests written in that language, some applications may produce standard print requests that may not be intelligible to PostScript printers. Examples of content types that may not be interpreted by some PostScript printers are shown in Figure 10-1.

Content Type	Type of Print Request
troff	Print output from a `troff` command.
simple	Print an ASCII file.
dmd	Print the contents of a bit-mapped display from a terminal such as an AT&T 630.
tek401	Print files formatted for a Tektronix 4014 device.
daisy	Print files intended for a Diablo 630 daisy-wheel printer.
plot	Print plot-formatted files

Figure 10-1: Non-Post-Script Print Requests
In general, Post-Script printers can print only PostScript files. Print requests with these contents types must use a filter that converts the data to PostScript.

Filters are provided with the LP print service to translate print requests with these formats to the PostScript language. For example, to convert a file containing ASCII text to PostScript code, the filter takes that text and writes a program around it, specifying printing parameters such as fonts and the layout of the text on a page.

Once the PostScript filters are installed, they will be invoked automatically by the LP print service when a user specifies a content-type for a print request with the -T option. For example, if a user enters the command

```
lp -d psprinter -T simple report2
```

the ASCII file `report2` (a file with an ASCII or `simple` format) will be converted to PostScript automatically, as long as the destination printer (`psprinter`) has been defined to the system as a PostScript printer.

❏ Providing Additional PostScript Capabilities With Filters

The PostScript filters provided with the LP print service take advantage of PostScript capabilities to provide additional printing flexibility. Most of these features may be accessed through the printing mode options of the `lp` command (the `-y` option). These filters allow you to use several unusual options for your print jobs. Figure 10-2 describes these options and shows the option you should include on the `lp` command line for each one.

Figure 10-2: Additional PostScript Printing Options. Filters are provided as part of the LP print services provide additional and unusual print options for the `lp` command. These options are all handled in the printer by the PostScript interpreter.

Option	Filter function
-y reverse	Reverse the order in which pages are printed .
-y landscape	Change the orientation of a physical page from portrait to landscape.
-y x=*number*, y=*number*	Change the default position of a logical page on a physical page by moving the origin.
-y group=*number*	Group multiple logical pages on a single physical page
-y magnify=*number*	Change the logical size of each page in a document.
-o length=*number*	Select the number of lines on each page of the document.
-P *number*	Select, by page numbers, a subset of a document to be printed.
-n *number*	Print multiple copies of a document

◆ *Note*

If these filters are to be used with an application that creates PostScript output, make sure that the format of the application conforms to the format of the PostScript file structuring comments. In particular, the beginning of each PostScript page must be marked by the comment

> `%%Page:` *label ordinal*

where *ordinal* is a positive integer that specifies the position of the page in the sequence of pages in the document, and *label* is an arbitrary page label.

Example - Landscape Mode Printing

Suppose you have a file called `report2` that has a content type `simple` (meaning that the content of this file is in ASCII format). You want to print six pages of this file (pages 4-9) with two logical pages on each physical page. Because one of the printers on your system (`psprinter`) is a PostScript printer, you can do this by entering the following command:

```
lp -d psprinter -T simple -P 4-9 -y group=2 myfile
```

The filter that groups these logical pages will try to position the pages on the physical page to maximize space utilization. Thus when you specify `group=2`, the pages will be printed side by side, so that the physical page will be landscape orientation. Landscape mode, which controls the orientation of the logical page rather than the physical page, would cause the logical pages to be positioned one on top of the other when combined with the `group=2` option.

❑ The Administrator's Duties

Support of PostScript printers is similar to support of other printers, in that the printers must be defined to the system with the `lpadmin` command and the appropriate software must be installed to manage them. PostScript printers may require some additional effort in supporting fonts.

Installing and Maintaining PostScript Printers

PostScript printers, like other printers, are installed with the `lpadmin` command. They must use the `PS` interface program, requested by specifying `-m PS` on the `lpadmin` command line.

◆ *Note*   The printer-type and content-type of a PostScript printer must be consistent with the printer type used in PostScript filters. Therefore you should install your PostScript printers with a printer-type of `PS` or `PSR`, and a content-type of `PS`.

The printer types PS and PSR serve two functions. First, they cause the print service to activate the postio filter to communicate with the printer. Second, the standard interface shell creates a PostScript banner page for printers with printer type PS or PSR. The banner page is printed last if the printer-type is PSR, and the pages of the document are printed in reverse order. The printer type is specified with the -T option in the lpadmin command.

As part of the installation, you may want to install fonts on the printer or downloadable fonts on the computer. See *Installing and Maintaining PostScript Fonts* later in this chapter for details.

Installing and Maintaining PostScript Filters

PostScript filters are provided with the LP print service add-on package and are installed during regular installation. This installation covers the majority of situations. In certain circumstances, however, you may find it helpful to change the filter descriptions and install the filters differently. To help you do this, this section describes the location and function of these filters.

PostScript filters are contained in the directory /usr/lib/lp/postscript.

 Note   There are two types of filters: fast filters and slow filters. For definitions of these types, see Chapter 9, *Filters*.

A prerequisite for communication between any system and a PostScript printer is the presence of the postio filter on the system. This program is the only mandatory PostScript filter that communicates directly with the PostScript printer. Figure 10-3 shows the names of the PostScript filters that are included with the LP print service and what they do.

Filter	Function
postpost	Convert simple files to PostScript
dpost	Convert troff files to PostScript
postdmd	Convert dmd files to PostScript
posttek	Convert tek4014 files to PostScript
postdaisy	Convert daisy files to PostScript
postplot	Convert plot files to PostScript
postio	Communicate with PostScript printers
download	Download fonts
postreverse	Reverse or select pages
postmd	Matrix grey scales

Figure 10-3: The Standard Post-Script Filters. These filters are included in the LP Print Service add-on package.

❏ Installing and Maintaining PostScript Fonts

One of the advantages of PostScript is its ability to manage fonts. Fonts are stored in outline form, either on the printer or on a computer that communicates with a printer. When a document is printed, the PostScript interpreter generates each character as needed (in the appropriate size) from the outline description of it. If a font required for a document is not stored on the printer being used, it must be transmitted to that printer before the document can be printed. This transmission process is called *downloading fonts*.

Fonts are stored and accessed in several ways.

▲ *Printer resident fonts* are stored permanently on a printer. They may be installed in ROM on the printer by the manufacturer, or, if the printer has a disk, fonts may be installed on that disk by the print service administrator. Most PostScript printers are shipped with thirty-five standard fonts.

▲ A font may be *permanently-downloaded* by being transmitted to a printer with a PostScript *exitserver* program. The font will remain in the printer's memory until the printer is turned off. Memory allocated to this font will reduce the memory available for PostScript print requests. Use of exitserver programs requires the printer system password and may be reserved for the printer administrator. This method is useful when there is continual use of a font by the majority of print requests serviced by that printer.

▲ Fonts may be prepended to a print request, and be transmitted as part of the print request. When the user's document has been printed, the space allocated to the font is freed for other print requests. The font is stored in the user's directory. This is the preferred method for fonts with more limited usage.

▲ *Host-resident fonts* are stored on a system shared by many users. This system may be a server for the printer or may be a system connected to the printer by a network. Each user requests specific fonts in the documents they print. This method is useful when there are a large number of available fonts or when there is not continual use of these fonts by all print requests. If the fonts will be used only on printers attached to a server, they should be stored on the server. If the fonts are to be used by users on one system, who may send jobs to multiple printers on a network, they may be stored on the users' system.

The LP print service allows you to manage fonts in any of these ways. It provides a special download filter to manage fonts using the last method described above.

The print service supplies `troff` width tables for the thirty-five standard PostScript fonts that reside on many PostScript printers, for use by the `troff` program.

❏ Managing Printer-Resident Fonts

Most PostScript printers come equipped with fonts resident in the printer ROM. Some printers have a disk on which additional fonts are stored. When a printer is installed, the list of printer-resident fonts should be added to the font-list for that printer. These lists are kept in the printer administration directories. For a particular printer, this list is contained in the file

`/etc/lp/printers/`*printer-name*`/residentfonts`

where *printer-name* is the name of the printer. When fonts are permanently downloaded to the printer, the font names should be added to this file. This will prevent fonts from being downloaded when they are already on the printer, a time-consuming procedure. If the printer is attached to a remote system, this list should include fonts that reside on that system and are available for downloading to the printer. This prevents fonts from being transmitted unnecessarily across a network. These files must be edited manually; that is, with the help of a text editor such as `vi`.

❑ Installing and Maintaining Host-Resident Fonts

Some fonts will be resident on the host and transmitted to the printer as needed for particular print requests. As the administrator, it's your job to make PostScript fonts available to all the users on a system. To do so, you must know how and where to install these fonts, using the guidelines described previously. Because fonts are requested by name and stored in files, the LP print service keeps a map file that shows the correspondence between the names of fonts and the names of the files containing those fonts. The map file must be updated when fonts are installed on the host.

Install host-resident PostScript fonts by doing the following:

▲ Copy the font file to the appropriate directory.

▲ Add to the map table the name of the font and the name of the file in which it resides.

▲ If you are using `troff`, you must create new width tables for this font in the standard `troff` font directory.

Where Are Fonts Stored?

The fonts available for use with PostScript printers reside in directories called `/usr/share/lib/hostfontdir/`*typeface*`/`*font* where *typeface* is replaced by a name such as `palatino` or `helvetica`, and *font* is replaced by a name such as `bold` or `italic`.

Adding an Entry to the Map Table

Also within the `hostfontdir` directory, you (the administrator) must create and maintain a map table that shows the correspondence between the name assigned to each font by the foundry (the company that created the font) and the name of the file in which that font resides. For example, to map the font called "Palatino Bold", add the following line to the map table:

```
Palatino-Bold /usr/share/lib/hostfontdir/palatino/bold
```

(The map table itself is in the file `/usr/share/lib/hostfontdir/map`).

Once this entry exists in the map table on your system, your users will be able to have a Palatino Bold font used in their print jobs. When they print a file containing a request for this font, the LP print service will prepend a copy of the file

```
/usr/share/lib/hostfontdir/palatino/bold
```

to that file before sending it to the printer.

❏ Downloading Host-Resident Fonts

The creators of the PostScript language anticipated that users would want to download fonts to printers. The *PostScript Language Reference Manual* [1] states the following:

"...programs that manage previously generated PostScript page descriptions, such as `printer spooler' utilities, may require additional information about those page descriptions. For example, if a page description references special fonts, a spooler may need to transmit definitions of those fonts to the PostScript printer ahead of the page description itself.

1. *PostScript Language Reference Manual*, Adobe Systems, Inc., Addison-Wesley Publishing Co., Inc., 1985

To facilitate these and other operations, [PostScript] defines a standard set of *structuring conventions* for PostScript programs."

The `download` filter relies on these structuring conventions to determine which fonts must be downloaded.

When a PostScript document contains a request for fonts not loaded on the printer, the `download` filter manages this request. This filter is invoked as a `fast` filter; it downloads fonts automatically if the fonts reside on the same system as the printer. The `download` filter can also be used to send fonts to a remote printer if you create a new filter table entry that calls the `download` filter as a `slow` filter through the `-y` option.

The `download` filter does five things:

▲ It searches the PostScript document to determine which fonts have been requested. These requests are documented with the following PostScript structuring comments:

    `%%DocumentFonts`: *font1 font2 ...*

in the header comments.

▲ It searches the list of fonts resident on that printer to see if the requested font must be downloaded.

▲ If the font is not resident on the printer, it searches the host-resident font directory (by getting the appropriate file name from the map table) to see if the requested font is available.

▲ If the font is available, the filter takes the file for that font and prepends it to the file to be printed.

▲ The filter sends the font definition file and the source file (the file to be printed) to the PostScript printer.

11

Troubleshooting

Here are a few suggestions of what to do if you are having difficulty getting a printer to work. The section headings each describe a symptom; the text in that section describes the potential problem. The list is by no means exhaustive.

❑ No Output

The printer is idle; nothing happens. First, check the documentation that came with the printer to see if there is a self-test feature you can invoke; make sure the printer is working before continuing.

Is the Printer Connected to the Computer?

The type of connection between a computer and a printer may vary. Verify that you have connected your printer correctly with the installation guide provided by the printer manufacturer.

Is the Printer Enabled?

The printer must be "enabled" in two ways: First, the printer must be turned on and ready to receive data from the computer. Second, the LP print service must be ready to use the printer. If you receive error messages when setting up your printer, follow the "fixes" suggested in the messages. When the printer is set up, issue the commands

```
accept  printer-name
enable  printer-name
```

where *printer-name* is the name you assigned to the printer for the LP print service. Now submit a sample file for printing:

```
lp  -d  printer-name file-name
```

Is the Baud Rate Correct?

If the baud rate (the rate at which data are transmitted) is not the same for both the computer and the printer, sometimes nothing will be printed (see below).

❑ Illegible Output

The printer tries printing, but the output is not what you expected; it certainly isn't readable.

Is the Baud Rate Correct?

Usually, when the baud rate of the computer doesn't match that of the printer, you'll get some output but it will not look at all like what you submitted for printing. Random characters will appear, with an unusual mixture of special characters and unlikely spacing. Read the documentation that came with the printer to find out what its baud rate is. It should probably be set at 9600 baud for optimum performance, but that doesn't matter for now. If it isn't set to 9600 baud, you can have the LP print service use the correct baud rate (by default it uses 9600). If the printer is connected through a parallel port, the baud rate is irrelevant.

To set a different baud rate for the LP print service, enter the following command:

```
lpadmin -p printer-name -o stty=baud-rate
```

Now submit a sample file for printing (explained earlier in this section).

Is the Parity Setting Correct?

Some printers use a "parity bit" to ensure that the data received for printing has not been garbled in transmission. The parity bit can be encoded in several ways; the computer and the printer must agree on which one to use. If they do not agree, some characters either will not be printed or will be replaced by other characters. Generally, though, the output will look approximately correct, with the spacing of "words" typical for your document and many letters in their correct place.

Check the documentation for the printer to see what the printer expects. The LP print service will not set the parity bit by default. You can change this, however, by entering one of the following commands:

```
lpadmin -p printer-name -o stty=oddp
lpadmin -p printer-name -o stty=evenp
lpadmin -p printer-name -o stty=-parity
```

The first command sets odd parity generation, the second sets even parity. The last command sets the default, no parity.

If you are also setting a baud rate other than 9600, you may combine the baud rate setting with the parity settings, as in the sample command below.

```
lpadmin -p printer-name -o "stty='evenp 1200'"
```

Both double and single quotes are necessary.

Are the Tabs Set Correctly?

If the printer doesn't expect to receive tab characters, the output may contain the complete content of the file, but the text may appear in a chaotic looking format, jammed up against the right margin (see below).

Is the Printer Type Correct?

See the *Wrong Character Set or Font* section below.

❏ Legible Printing, but Wrong Spacing

The output contains all of the expected text and may be readable, but the text appears in an undesirable format:

- ▲ double spaced,
- ▲ with no left margin,
- ▲ run together, or
- ▲ zig-zagging down the page.

These problems can be fixed by adjusting the printer settings (if possible) or by having the LP print service use settings that match those of the printer. The rest of this section provides details about solving each of these types of problems.

Double Spaced

Either the printer's tab settings are wrong or the printer is adding a linefeed after each carriage return. (The LP print service has a carriage return added to each linefeed, so the combination causes two linefeeds.) You can have the LP print service not send tabs or not add a carriage return by using the `stty -tabs` option or the `-onlcr` option, respectively.)

```
lpadmin -p printer-name -o stty=-tabs
lpadmin -p printer-name -o stty=-onlcr
```

No Left Margin/Runs Together/Jammed Up

The printer's tab settings aren't correct; they should be set every 8 spaces. You can have the LP print service not send tabs by using the -tabs option.

```
lpadmin -p printer-name -o stty=-tabs
```

Zig Zags Down the Page

The stty onlcr option is not set. This is set by default, but you may have cleared it accidentally.

```
lpadmin -p printer-name -o stty=onlcr
```

A Combination of Problems

If you need to use several of these options to take care of multiple problems, you can combine them in one list, as shown in the sample command below. Include any baud rate or parity settings, too.

```
lpadmin -p printer-name -o "stty='-onlcr -tabs 2400'"
```

Correct Printer Type?

See below.

❑ Wrong Character Set or Font

If the wrong printer type was selected when you set up the printer with the LP print service, the wrong "control characters" can be sent to the printer. The results are unpredictable and may cause output to disappear or to be illegible, making it look like the result of one of the problems described above. Another result may be that the wrong control characters cause the printer to set the wrong character set or font.

If you don't know which printer type to specify, try the following to examine the available printer types. First, if you think the printer type has a certain name, try the following command:

```
tput -T printer-type longname
```

(This may not work on early versions of UNIX System V.) The output of this command will appear on your terminal: a short description of the printer identified by the *printer-type*. Try the names you think might be right until you find one that identifies your printer.

If you don't know what names to try, you can examine the `terminfo` directory to see what names are available. Warning: There are probably many names in that directory. Enter the following command to examine the directory.

```
ls -R /usr/share/lib/terminfo/*
```

Pick names from the list that match one word or number identifying your printer. For example, the name `495` would identify the AT&T 495 Printer. Try each of the names in the other command above.

When you have the name of a printer type you think is correct, set it in the LP print service by entering the following command:

```
lpadmin -p printer-name -T printer-type
```

❏ Dial Out Failures

The LP print service uses the Basic Network Utilities (BNU) to handle dial out printers. If a dialing failure occurs and you are receiving printer fault alerts, the LP print service reports the same error reported by the BNU software for similar problems. (If you haven't arranged to receive fault alerts, they are mailed, by default, to the user `lp`.) Look up the error messages in the manuals that came with the Basic Network Utilities package.

Idle Printers

There are several reasons why you may find a printer idle and enabled but with print requests still queued for it:

▲ The print requests need to be filtered. Slow filters run one at a time to avoid overloading the system. Until a print request has been filtered (if it needs slow filtering), it will not print. Use the following command to see if the first waiting request is being filtered.

```
lpstat -o -l
```

▲ The printer has a fault. After a fault has been detected, printing resumes automatically, but not immediately. The LP print service waits about five minutes before trying again, and continues trying until a request is printed successfully. You can force a retry immediately by enabling the printer as follows:

```
enable printer-name
```

▲ A dial out printer is busy or doesn't answer, or all dial out ports are busy. As with automatic continuation after a fault, the LP print service waits five minutes before trying to reach a dial out printer again. If the dial out printer can't be reached for an hour or two (depending on the reason), the LP print service finally alerts you to a possible problem. You can force a retry immediately by enabling the printer as follows:

```
enable printer-name
```

▲ A "child process" is lost. If the UNIX process controlling the printer is killed (by the UNIX system during periods of extremely heavy load or by a system administrator), the LP print service may not realize it for a few minutes. Disabling the printer and then reenabling it again will force the print service to check for the controlling process and restart one. Make sure that the printer is really idle, though, because disabling a busy printer stops it in the middle of printing a request. The request will not be lost, but it will be reprinted in its entirety.

```
disable printer-name
enable printer-name
```

If the last process is one controlling a slow filter, don't try to reenable the printer. Put the request at the head of the queue on hold, instead, and then resume it:

```
lpstat -o -l
lp -i request -H hold
```

```
lp -i request -H resume
```

(The first command lists the queued requests so that you can choose
the right value for *request*.)

❑ Networking Problems

You may encounter several types of problems while trying to get files printed
over a network:

1. Requests being sent to remote printers may back up in the local
   queue.

2. Requests sent to remote printers may be backed up in the remote
   queue.

3. A user may receive contradictory messages about whether a remote
   printer has accepted a print request.

The rest of this section describes each of these situations and suggests how to
resolve them.

Jobs Backing Up in the Local Queue

There are a lot of jobs backing up in the local queue for a remote printer. There
are three possible explanations:

▲ The remote system is down or the network between the local and
  remote systems is down. To resolve this problem, run the `reject`
  command for all the remote printers on your system, as follows:

  ```
  reject printer-name
  ```

  This will stop new requests for those printers from being added to the
  queue. Once the system comes up again, and jobs start being taken
  from your queue, type

  ```
  accept printer-name
  ```

  to allow new jobs to be queued.

▲ The remote printer is disabled on the local system.

▲   The underlying network software was not set up properly. See Chapter 2, *Installing the LP Print Service*, and your network services installation guide.

Jobs Backing Up in the Remote Queue

The remote printer has been disabled.

Conflicting Messages about the Acceptance/Rejection of Jobs

A user enters a print request and is notified that the system has accepted it. The job is sent to a remote system and the user receives mail that the job has been rejected. This may be happening for one of two reasons. First, the local computer may be accepting requests while the remote computer is rejecting requests.

Second, the definition of the remote printer on the local computer may not match the definition of that printer on the remote computer. Specifically, the definitions of print job components such as filters, character sets, print wheels, and forms are not the same on the local and remote systems. Identical definitions of these job components must be registered on both the local and the remote systems, if local users are to be able to access remote printers.

Quick Reference Guide to Print Service Administration

These commands are found in the `/usr/lib` directory. (If you expect to use them frequently, you might find it convenient to include that directory in your PATH variable. To use the administrative commands, you must be logged in either as `root` or as `lp`. You'll also probably need to use the commands for disabling and enabling a printer and the rest of the user commands.

Administrative Task	Command	See Chapters
Activating a printer	enable	3, 6
Canceling a request for a file to be printed	cancel	5
Deactivating a specified printer(s)	disable	5
Mounting a form or printwheel	lpadmin	3, 4, 7
Moving output requests from one destination to another	lpmove	5, 6
Permitting job requests to be queued for a specific destination	accept	3, 5, 6
Preventing jobs from being queued for a specified destination	reject	5, 6
Reporting the status of the LP print service	lpstat	6, 7
Sending a file (or files) to a printer	lp	6, 9
Setting up or changing printer configurations	lpadmin	3, 4
Setting up or changing filter definitions	lpfilter	8, 9
Setting up or changing pre-printed forms	lpforms	7
Setting or changing the default priority and priority limits that can be requested by users of the LP print service	lpusers	6
Starting the LP print service scheduler	lpsched	5
Stopping the LP print service scheduler	lpshut	5

Glossary

allow list   A list of users allowed to use a printer or a pre-printed form. See Chapter 3, *Configuring Printers*, and Chapter 8, *Pre-printed Forms*, for information on creating an allow list.

application   The software designed to perform a specific task. For example, you use a spreadsheet application to manipulate columns and rows of numbers and a word processing application to create, edit, and format printed pages.

class   A group of equivalent printers. Classes are defined using `lpadmin` and can be used to establish a priority ordering of equivalent printers. See Chapter 3, *Configuring Printers*, and Chapter 4, *Using Menus to Configure Printers*, for directions on creating and managing printer classes.

client   A remote system that desires access to the printers on a server.

command   An instruction that tells a computer to perform a specific function or to carry out a specific activity.

content type   A description of the format of a print file. Printers can print some content types directly; others must be filtered before being printed. See Chapter 3, *Configuring Printers*, for more information on creating a content type list for a printer, and Chapter 9, *Filters*, for information on filters that can convert files from one content type to another.

daemon   A program that runs as a background process to handle UNIX system activities. Examples are the LP print service scheduler, `lpsched`, and `crontab`, which can be used to clean out the print request logs.

default   The value that is used if no value is specified.

deny list   A list of users that are denied access to a printer or a pre-printed form. See Chapter 3, *Configuring Printers*, and Chapter 8, *Pre-printed Forms*, for information on creating a deny list.

distributed printing configuration
                   A system configuration in which each computer has a direct connection to a printer.

downloading fonts
                   The process of transmitting a font to a printer. Printer-resident fonts need not be downloaded. A host-resident font can be down-loaded by prepending it to each print request that requires it, or by "permanently" downloading it with an exit-server.

draft quality   Lower resolution but more quickly and/or less expensively produced. Some dot matrix printers can print "quick and dirty" drafts or "nice and slow" final versions.

error message   A response from a program indicating that a problem has arisen or that something unexpected has happened and requires your attention.

exit code   A numeric code set by the interface program that indicates that completion status of a print request. Zero means successful completion; any other value indicates a problem. Figure 5-6 in Chapter 5, *Customizing the Print Service*, shows the correspondence between exit codes and printer problems.

exitserver   A program used to "permanently" download fonts to a PostScript printer. The font is stored in printer memory, thus reducing the amount of space available for page composition. The font will reside in memory and be accessible to print jobs until the printer is turned off.

filter   A program that processes the data in a file before it is printed. Filters can convert data from one output format to another, implement unusual printing options like reversing the pages or printing in landscape mode, and can catch and recover from printer faults. Fast filters send their output directly to a printer (or another fast filter); slow filters send their output to a file (or another slow filter) to avoid tying up a printer for a long time. See Chapter 9, *Filters*, for information about customizing existing filters and creating new ones.

form   Paper that is already printed with text and graphics that can be loaded into a printer instead of plain paper. Examples are letterhead, blank checks, invoices, and labels. See Chapter 8, *Pre-printed Forms*.

host-resident fonts
    Fonts that are stored on a system shared by many users. The fonts are generally accessible and can be prepended to any print request that requires them.

interface program
    A program that sets the printer up for a print request. It may locate and prepend host-resident fonts, gang filters together to form a pipeline of fast filters that feeds data to the printer, and examine the exit code when the printing is complete.

landscape mode
    A printing mode where pages are wider than they are tall, like a typical painting of a landscape.

letter quality   High-quality printing - the kind you wouldn't be ashamed to print on your letterhead and sign your name to.

local printer   A printer that is directly connected to a system on which its print requests originate.

modem   A device that modulates and demodulates data transmitted over communication lines.

network printing configuration

A system configuration in which printers can be located on a server or distributed across a network of computers, or both. The printers are generally accessible to all users on the network, regardless of which system they are connected to.

option

An addition to a command to improve or enhance the function. The option is usually indicated by a – followed by a key letter and arguments, if any.

pathname

The path through the file system tree that is specified to identify a file. An *absolute pathname* starts from the root directory /. A *relative pathname* starts from the current directory.

pipeline

Two or more commands connected with the pipe operator |. The standard output of the first command becomes the standard input of the next command, and so on. Pipelines are uni-directional.

portrait mode

A printing mode where pages are taller than they are wide - like a typical portrait.

PostScript

A programming language with special features for describing the appearance of both text and graphics on a page. A PostScript printer contains a computer and a PostScript interpreter that converts PostScript programs into printed pages. See Chapter 10, *PostScript Printers*, for information about supporting PostScript and PostScript printers.

print server configuration

A system configuration in which several printers are connected to a single computer and users on other systems access the printers across a network.

printer-resident fonts

Fonts that are stored permanently on a printer. These may be in ROM by the manufacturer, or, if the printer has a local disk, installed on the disk by the print service administrator. Most PostScript printers are shipped with 35 printer-resident fonts.

remote printer   A printer that is connected to a system accessible across a network.

server   A computer that has several printers directly connected and provides printing services to remote users.

spooling   An acronym for **s**imultaneous **p**eripheral **o**peration **o**n-**l**ine. The LP print service spools output so that users can continue working while the print request is processed.

Index

Notes

Notes

Notes

Notes

Notes

Notes

Notes

Notes

Notes

Notes

Notes

Notes